THE EVERYTHING KIDS' GROSS

Puzzle & Activity Book

Hours of disgusting fun!

Beth L. Blair and Jennifer A. Ericsson

Adams Media

Avon, Massachusetts

EDITORIAL
Publishing Director: Gary M. Krebs
Associate Managing Editor: Laura M. Daly
Associate Copy Chief: Brett Palana-Shanahan
Acquisitions Editor: Kate Burgo
Associate Production Editor: Casey Ebert

PRODUCTION
Director of Manufacturing: Susan Beale
Associate Director of Production: Michelle Roy Kelly
Cover Design: Paul Beatrice, Erick DaCosta, Matt LeBlanc
Design and Layout: Colleen Cunningham,
    Holly Curtis, Erin Dawson, Sorae Lee

An Everything® Series Book.
Everything® and everything.com® are registered trademarks of F+W Publications, Inc.

Published by Adams Media, an F+W Publications Company
57 Littlefield Street, Avon, MA 02322. U.S.A.
www.adamsmedia.com

ISBN: 1-59337-447-X

Printed in the United States of America.

J   I   H   G   F   E   D   C   B   A

Cover and Interior illustrations by Kurt Dolber.
Puzzles by Beth L. Blair.

This book is available at quantity discounts for bulk purchases.
For information, please call 1-800-872-5627.

See the entire Everything® series at *www.everything.com*.

Contents

Introduction

Warning! Warning!

This book is totally GROSS!

Gross?

Yes, Gross. You know . . . disgusting, vulgar, possibly even shocking. Parts of it will certainly make you scrunch up your face and yell "EEEW! THAT'S GROSS!"

Are you still reading?

Then you must find gross things fascinating. Maybe you think snot is swell. Perhaps you find tarantulas tasty. You may even think that maggots are marvelous! Well, if grossness is your thing, then you'll definitely love this book.

We've created nine chapters of great puzzles covering icky topics like Body Badness, Bathroom Humor, Awful Animals, Foul Food, and Medical Madness. Just as each person has their own tolerance for gross stuff, they also have their own taste in the kind of puzzles they like to do. Throughout the book there are a ton of mazes, word searches, acrostics, hidden pictures, dot-to-dots, and many other types of puzzles. We know there is something here to happily gross out every kind of kid!

Also, as you puzzle your way through the book, you might be surprised to find that many of the gross topics included are, in fact, historical, comical, or even useful! Be on the lookout for the "Gross, but true!" facts and, if you still haven't had enough by the time you are done with all the puzzles, there is a great list of books and Web sites so you can continue to be engrossed with gross.

So get ready, get set, get GROSS!

Start out by breaking this VOWEL SCRAMBLE Code:

Gotcha thinking gross!

Beth L. Blair and Jennifer A. Ericsson

Knick, Knick.
Whi's thara?
Wutsin.
Wutsin whi?
**Wutsin yior nisa?
Et liiks leka u beg
ild biigar!!**

DEDICATION

Jennifer and Beth ~ friends since childhood ~ dedicate this gross book to each other. "Remember, you can pick your friends, and you can pick your nose, but you can't pick your friend's nose!"

What do you get when you cross a skunk, an owl, and a mountain?

To find the answer to this riddle, think of a word that best fits each of the descriptions below. Write the words on the numbered lines, and then transfer each letter into the numbered grid. The black boxes are the spaces between words.

A. Says "BOO"

<u>G</u> <u>H</u> <u>O</u> <u>S</u> <u>T</u>
42 47 48 1 50

B. To cast a ballot

_ _ _ _
44 49 5 4

C. A small clue

_ _ _ _
22 23 31 41

D. To push hard

_ _ _ _ _
19 25 37 29 27

E. Opposite of fat

_ _ _ _
10 6 43 40

F. To put up a picture

_ _ _ _
11 12 17 24

G. A precious jewel

_ _ _
9 30 3

H. Cousin of a frog

_ _ _ _
13 2 46 35

I. Bugs at a picnic

_ _ _ _
28 8 15 14

J. Do, Re, or Me

_ _ _ _
34 21 20 45

K. Past tense of SAY

_ _ _ _
32 33 7 36

L. Long walks

_ _ _ _ _
26 16 18 38 39

1A S	2H	3G	4B	5B	6E	7K	8I	9G		
10 E	11 F	12 F	13 H		14 I	15 I	16 L	17 F	18 L	19 D
	20 J	21 J		22 C	23 C	24 F	25 D			
26 L	27 D	28 I	29 D	30 G	31 C	32 K		33 K	34 J	35 H
	36 K	37 D	38 L	39 L	40 E	41 C				
42 A G	43 E	44 B	45 J		46 H		47 A H	48 A O	49 B	50 A T

2

Pillow P.U.

What do you call a tiny, magical being who farts under your pillow?

To find out, connect the dots. Then, put a penny on each of the two dots without numbers. Trace around them to complete the picture.

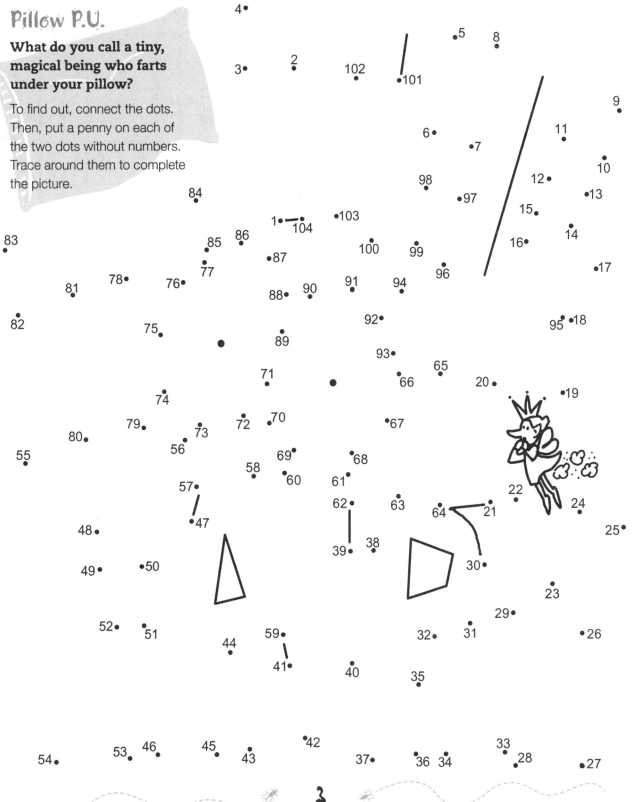

What did the mad scientist say when he finally created a smelly monster?

To find out what the scientist said, use a dark color marker or pencil to color in all the boxes with the letters S-M-E-L-L-Y.

S	B	C	A	M	S	E	S	L	S	L	M	Y	E	S	L	C	B
A	S	H	F	E	A	M	C	E	B	C	Y	C	L	B	L	H	G
F	E	W	J	L	F	B	H	D	G	H	A	H	A	G	Y	W	K
J	G	M	O	L	J	G	M	I	K	W	F	M	F	K	S	Q	S
O	K	Q	T	S	O	K	E	S	P	Q	E	L	J	P	M	V	P
T	P	V	S	M	T	P	L	M	U	V	L	E	O	U	E	S	U
S	M	D	M	A	X	U	W	N	Z	A	J	W	T		A	M	Z
X	U	I	E	L	Z	Q	R	E	S	O	Q		Z	L	E	A
B	Z	N	X	L	B	V	W	A	F	T		X	C	L	D	F
G	E	E	B	Y	G	C	D	S	L	M	L	V	B	H	Y	I	G
K	L	R	G	F	S	Y	I	A	F	J	X	A	S	E	F	L	O
P	L	W	K	J	K	H	Y	M	L	E	Y	E	G	W	C	L	T
S	B	C	D	S	A	B	D	S	A	C	L	X	Q	A	D	I	S
A	G	H	S	D	F	G	M	M	F	H	L	S	W	E	M	N	M
F	K	W	I	W	J	K	I	E	S	S	E	A	R	G	E	R	A
M	P	S	N	M	S	M	N	A	J	W	Z	F	T	O	L	E	J
E	U	M	R	E	A	E	R	L	O	Q	S	J	D	T	I	Y	G
L	S	E	W	L	F	L	W	L	T	V	M	O	I	X	N	W	E
J	M	G	A	L	J	S	A	Y	X	B	E	T	N	X	R	A	G
O	E	K	F	Y	M	E	B	S	M	E	L	P	R	T	W	B	O
T	Z	P	G	Q	A	B	C	B	D	H	Z	P	W	O	D	C	T
L	L	S	O	E	M	G	E	S	I	L	W	M	Q	A	S	E	L
Y	C	M	T	L	F	K	L	C	N	L	N	E	A	G	M	Q	L
S	L	A	X	L	E	P	L	S	R	M	L	N		E	Y	S
M	H	L	Q	S	J	U	Y	D	W	Y	B	S	B	W	L	Z	Y
S	W	E	R	M	L	Z	E	L	Q	E	G	E	C	Q	L	Q	E

4

Officially Bad Breath

Believe it or not, scientists have a special word for stinky breath! To learn what it is, unscramble the words to the right. They are all things that can give you a smelly mouth. Write the unscrambled words on the dotted lines, and read the shaded letters from top to bottom.

LIHIC   _ _ _ _ _

STIVACIE   _ _ _ _ _ _ _ _

QUELAP   _ _ _ _ _ _

CLIRAG   _ _ _ _ _ _

RATRAT   _ _ _ _ _ _

FEEFOC   _ _ _ _ _ _

SNIOON   _ _ _ _ _ _

FINSECTION   _ _ _ _ _ _ _ _ _ _

MOGINKS   _ _ _ _ _ _ _

Do what?!?

Everyone knows that brushing and flossing are good ways to get rid of bad breath. There's something unexpected that also helps! Work your way through the maze picking up letters as you go. Write the letters down in order to reveal another way to clean up a messy mouth.

GROSS, BUT TRUE!

Ancient Egyptians used a toothpaste made from ox hooves and eggshells (first burned, and then ground up), mixed with myrrh (a spice), and pumice (grit).

FRANK

FREDD

Fart Foods

Frank and Fredd want to have a farting contest. They have each chosen foods known to make people get tooting. Use the Fart Foods list, below, to see who has the highest score, and will toot more!

Apple Pie *(with cheese)*
Grilled Cheese
Baked Beans
Radishes

Cheese Pizza
Cauliflower
　(with cheese sauce)
Large Cola
Steamed Broccoli
Bean Soup

milk = 1
apples = 2
cheese = 3
onions = 4
radishes = 5
soda = 6
beans = 7
broccoli = 8
cabbage = 9

brussels
sprouts = 10

cauliflower
= 11

Onion Rings

Coleslaw

Milkshake

GROSS, BUT TRUE!

A fart is not a burp that went the wrong way. The chemicals that make up a fart are different than those that make up a burp!

Mon.	
Tues.	
Wed.	
Thurs.	
Fri.	
Sat.	
Sun.	

Fart Chart

Most people fart about 14 times a day. Keep track of the number of times you fart each day for a whole week. Add up all the farts, then divide that number by 7 to find the average number of farts per day.

How do you rate? Are you a "Tiny Tooter" or a "Gale Force"?

GROSS, BUT TRUE!

If you hold in a fart, it doesn't just disappear. It bubbles back up into your intestines, and comes out again later!

_____ ÷ 7 = _____
total farts *farts per day*

1-3	Tiny Tooter
4-7	Big Wind
8-10	Thunderstorm
11-14	Gale Force
15+	Class 5 Hurricane

Stink Pinks

The answers to Stink Pinks are two rhyming words that each have one syllable. Use the clues to figure these out!

An intelligent toot

_ _ _ _ _   _ _ _ _

Seven days of smelliness

_ _ _ _   _ _ _ _ _

A fish fart

_ _ _ _   _ _ _

A hard, quick sniff

_ _ _ _ _   _ _ _ _ _

Smell from a moldy camping shelter

_ _ _ _   _ _ _ _ _ _

An apple passing gas

_ _ _ _ _   _ _ _ _ _

Smelly odor from a liquid you might swallow

_ _ _ _ _   _ _ _ _

Disgusting Dump

It doesn't take much to make a whole can-full of trash smell pretty putrid. Can you find a used diaper, a slimy banana peel, a rotten egg, a half-eaten chicken leg, a bunch of stinky fish bones, moldy wheel of cheese, moldy slice of bread, a dirty sock, and an old onion? For extra "fun," how many cartons of sour chocolate milk can you count?

Funky Fertilizer

These two farmers are having quite a conversation about their cows' stinky manure. To see what they are saying to each other, figure out where each puzzle piece goes in the empty grids. Then, write the letters in their proper places.

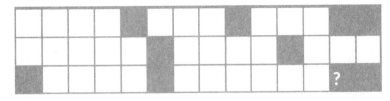

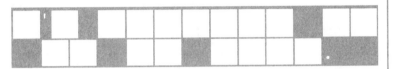

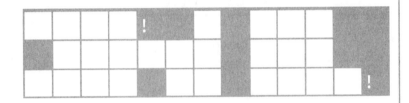

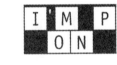

9

Smelling Sweet?

Change the word SWEET into the word SMELL one letter at a time. For each step, definitions have been provided as clues to the new word.

HINT: Letters might change position from step to step, but only one of the letters will be new.

SWEET	tastes like sugar
	salty body fluid
	to say curse words
	sharp, pointy weapon
	to utter words
	to slap on the butt
	past tense of stink
	main stem of a plant
	horse's room in a barn
	formal form of "will"
	hard outer covering
SMELL	to use your nose

Smell vs. Smell

A certain item has been used throughout history to cover up the smell of unwashed bodies, dirty clothes, and rank rooms. What is it? Place the words in alphabetical order from top to bottom. Read the answer down the shaded boxes.

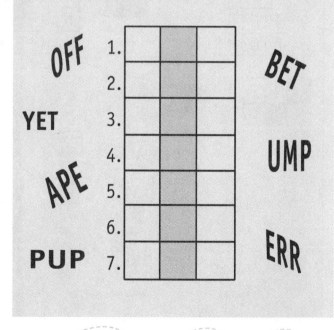

OFF   BET

YET   UMP

APE

PUP   ERR

1.
2.
3.
4.
5.
6.
7.

Super Sweat

Do you know what part of your body sweats the most? To find out, circle the letters that appear only once.

GROSS, BUT TRUE!

On a hot day, your body can make up to four cups of sweat!

It Was the Dog!

START

Travel from START to FART to find out which innocent-looking character really passed the gas.

fart

fart

Ode to Odor

Choose words from the list to complete this rancid rhyme in praise of dirty socks!

_____ socks, they never get _____.

The _____ you _____ them,

the _____ they get!

_____ falls, you _____

of the _____ , but

_____ inside you

says, "Don't _____ them yet!"

**LAUNDRY
DIRTY
BLACK
WASH
WEAR
BLACKER
DREAM
LONGER
NIGHT
SOMETHING**

EXTRA FUN:
Try filling in this poem using totally different words. Or, try changing the lyrics of a favorite song to make them smellier!

Stinky Socks

Which socks smell the worst? To find out, use the pattern code to count up the points.

GROSS, BUT TRUE!
The Guinness Book of Records lists a researcher who has sniffed over 5,600 pairs of feet!

thin stripes = 2 pts. each
polka dots = 3 pts. each

diamonds = 4 pts. each
fat stripes = 5 pts. each

X-tremely Gross

Our bodies can be really gross! Figure out the words suggested by the clues below, and fit them into the grid on the next page. We left a few I-C-K-Y F-A-T B-O-O-G-E-R-S to help.

ACROSS

2. Sound your body makes after a big meal or a fizzy drink.

5. Itchy skin bumps caused by an allergy.

7. When you have the flu, you feel really _____.

10. Crusty covering for a cut.

12. Red, itchy spots all over your skin.

14. Drinking water or holding your breath will sometimes stop these.

15. Another word for GROSS.

16. A hot, red swelling under the skin filled with pus.

18. Another word for "dirt."

19. A brown spot on your skin. Sometimes it's hairy.

20. Most people fart approximately 14 times a _____.

25. Dry flakes of skin from your scalp.

26. Sometimes when your mouth waters, it's a _____ that you're about to throw up.

28. Sweaty hollow under your arm.

30. Another word for GROSS.

32. It is impossible to keep your eyes open when your body does this!

34. A short way to say "That hurt!"

35. More common word for "saliva."

41. Your mouth is where a burp _____ from your body.

42. Another word for "booger."

43. Salty fluid that squirts from your eyes when you smell onions.

44. Wet and sticky, like your eyeball.

45. On a really hot day, your skin _____.

46. Another word that means someone is "smelly."

DOWN

1. A body part that often gets bruised against furniture.

3. Nasty, blood-sucking bugs that can make your scalp all itchy.

4. Another name for a germ that can make you feel gross.

6. The proper word for "hurl."

8. The official name for the slimy fluid in your mouth, nose, and throat.

9. Broken, leaky blood vessels under your skin makes one of these purple blotches.

11. The lump of nerves, blood vessels, body fluid, and tissue inside your skull.

13. The skin on your palms is hairless, but the skin on your head is _____.

16. What gushes out of a nasty cut.

17. Common name for the gunk between your toes. You don't want this on toast!

21. Squishy bubble of liquid on the skin.

22. Believe it or not, this is the strongest muscle in your body!

23. Bumpy growth on your skin caused by a virus, not a toad.

24. Another word for GROSS.

27. When your mom says "You have potatoes in your ears!", she's really talking about this stuff.

29. Yellowish-white liquid that oozes from an infection.

31. Another way to say "smells really bad."

33. Another word for GROSS.

36. Short way of saying "That stinks!"

37. What every kid calls "pimples."

38. In some parts of the world, people eat a kind of _____ made with vegetables, broth, and jelly-fish. Gross!

39. This is your body's largest organ. Hint: It sweats a lot!

40. When you have a really bad cold, snot may _____ out of your nose.

41. A cyclops has only one _____.

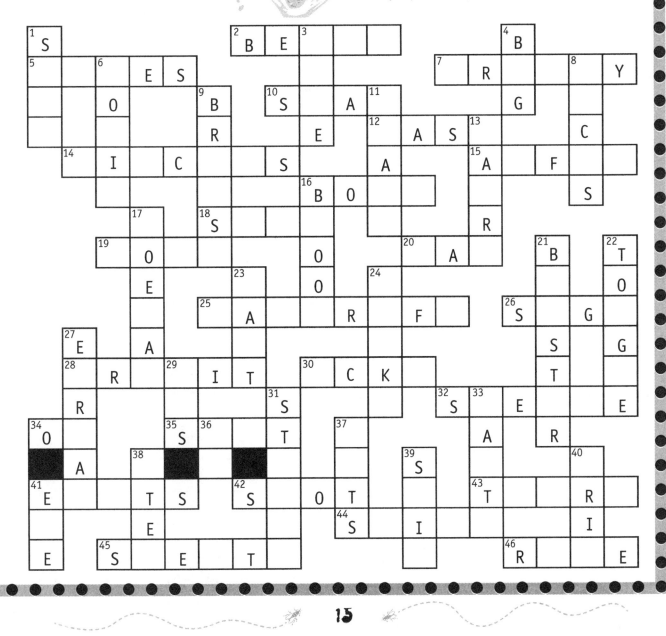

Slop Talk

Yuck! Can you grab the slippery letters and fit them into the blanks to create five words? All these words will rhyme with each other, and one of them is a common name for "saliva"!

1. _ _ _ _ _
2. _ _ _ _ _
3. _ _ _ _ _
4. _ _ _ _ _
5. _ _ _ _ _

Ah-Zoom!

How many miles-per-hour can a sneeze explode out of your nose? To find out, unscramble the eight sneeze-causing words below. Fit the answers into the grid and read down the shaded column. We left a bit of S-N-O-T to help you out!

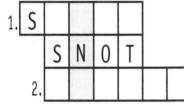

7. NEOPLL
6. YRELALG
3. TILGH
5. DOCL
8. LOMD
2. EREPPP
1. EOSMK
4. TUDS

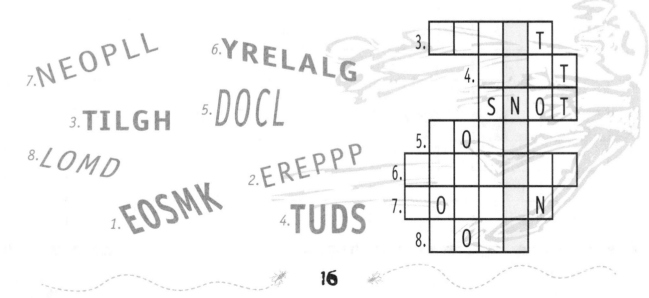

16

Dust and Decay

Most of the dust in your house is made up of one particular part of your body. To find out what that is, start at the number one in each of the three sections of this puzzle, and and connect the dots in order.

HINT: Connect the dots with swooping, curved lines—as if you were writing cursive!

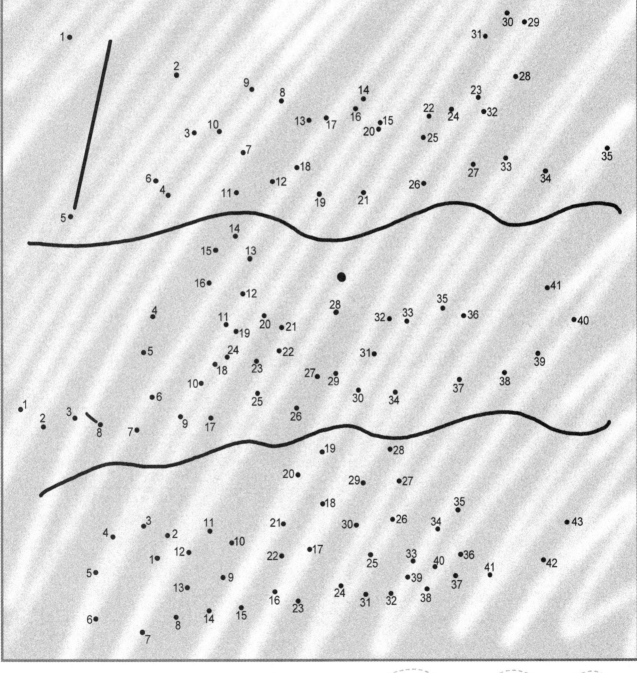

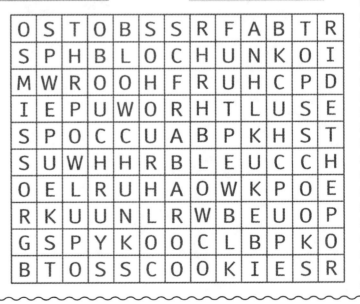

GROSS
#1 + OPPOSITE OF ME + (key) -Y

SNAKE NOISE + GROSS #1 + FEMALE SHEEP

Vomit Vocab

Everybody vomits, but not everyone calls it the same thing! See if you can figure out the following picture puzzles and word equations. Each one will either spell or act out some familiar vomit vocabulary. How many of these phrases do you use?

EXTRA FUN: See if you can find the answers hidden in the word search!

O	S	T	O	B	S	S	R	F	A	B	T	R
S	P	H	B	L	O	C	H	U	N	K	O	I
M	W	R	O	O	H	F	R	U	H	C	P	D
I	E	P	U	W	O	R	H	T	L	U	S	E
S	P	O	C	C	U	A	B	P	K	H	S	T
S	U	W	H	H	R	B	L	E	U	C	C	H
O	E	L	R	U	H	A	O	W	K	P	O	E
R	K	U	U	N	L	R	W	B	E	U	O	P
G	S	P	Y	K	O	O	C	L	B	P	K	O
B	T	O	S	S	C	O	O	K	I	E	S	R

True or False

Read the following statements about your body. Some of them are True and some of them are False. Circle your answer, then check in the back of the book to see if you're right!

1. You have as many hairs on your body as a gorilla.
   TRUE or FALSE

2. Your skull protects your brain so it can't be bruised.
   TRUE or FALSE

3. Cracking your knuckles can lead to arthritis.
   TRUE or FALSE

4. If you hold in a burp, it will become a fart.
   TRUE or FALSE

5. Boogers are very clean.
   TRUE or FALSE

6. Fresh spit is cleaner than fresh pee.
   TRUE or FALSE

7. The scientific name for snot is mucus.
   TRUE or FALSE

8. You will shed 40 pounds of skin in your lifetime.
   TRUE or FALSE

Grossly Gifted

The Guinness Book of Records lists a guy who can blow spaghetti out his nose! How many inches did he shoot a spaghetti strand to earn this honor? Complete the equations below to find out.

$$4 + 6 - 5\tfrac{1}{2} = \underline{\hspace{2cm}}$$

$$7 - 6 + \tfrac{1}{2} - 2 = \underline{\hspace{2cm}}$$

$$3 + 1\tfrac{1}{2} - 4\tfrac{1}{2} = \underline{\hspace{2cm}}$$

$$6 - 4\tfrac{1}{2} + 1 = \underline{\hspace{2cm}}$$

$$9\tfrac{1}{2} - 8 - \tfrac{1}{2} = \underline{\hspace{2cm}}$$

Total inches = \underline{\hspace{2cm}}

Edible Earwax

Here's an easy way to make a gross-out treat for your next party. Don't wait for Halloween—earwax is good to eat any time of year!

You will need:
An adult to help with the oven
1 tube ready-bake sugar cookie dough
1 small jar of apricot preserves
½ cup golden (not brown) raisins
dinner knife
teaspoon
spatula
oven-mitts

1. Read the directions on the tube of sugar cookie dough, and ask your adult helper to preheat the oven to 350°.

2. Together with your helper, slice the cookie dough into slices about ¼ inch thick. Cut each circular slice in half, and place on an ungreased cookie sheet, about 2 inches apart. Take a pinch of dough and roll it into a ball the size of a marble. Stick a dough ball on the bottom edge of each half circle.

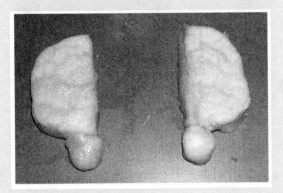

3. Poke your fingertip into each "ear" to make a hole for the earwax.

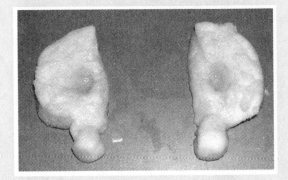

4. Fill the hole with a very small scoop of apricot preserves, about ¼ teaspoon. Stick one or two raisins in the preserves.

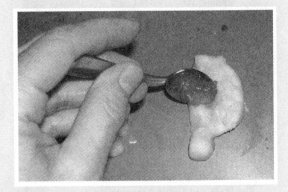

5. Bake ears for 11 minutes, until golden brown all over and puffy.

6. Have your helper take the cookies out of the oven. While the cookies are still on the cookie sheet, and still hot, take a metal teaspoon and gently press the tip into the cookie to make the shape of the ridges in the ear. We think it looks best to make two ridges, one close to the edge of the ear, and a smaller ridge in close to the earwax.

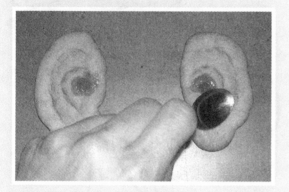

7. Use a spatula to slide the ears off the cookie sheet. Cool on a wire rack. This recipe will make at least 18 pairs of ears with wax. YUM!

What Smells?

You can almost read the joke below, but something isn't quite right! Figure out which letters have been switched to see what these two stinkers are really talking about.

Stenky: Thasa pells E git ti gat red if B.I. din't wirk.

Penky: Why nit?

Stenky: Thay kaap fulleng iot frim ondar my urms!

Acne Art

Artie has a horrible case of zits! But if you connect them all in order by number, the end result is rather cool.

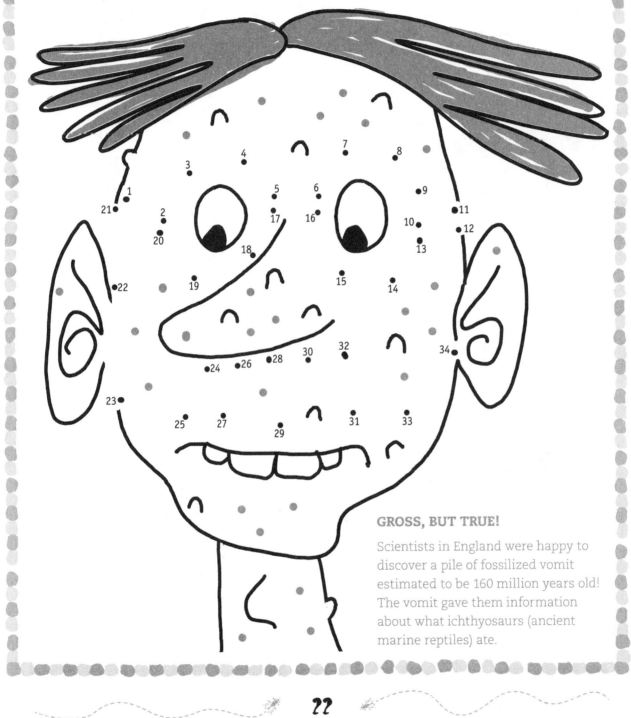

GROSS, BUT TRUE!

Scientists in England were happy to discover a pile of fossilized vomit estimated to be 160 million years old! The vomit gave them information about what ichthyosaurs (ancient marine reptiles) ate.

Pus-itively Putrid

You get a cut, it gets dirty, it gets hot and red and suddenly there's a lot of icky, yellowish-white pus gooshing around in there. This is a sure sign that your body is fighting off an infection, but what is that gross and goopy pus made of? Use a reverse letter substitution code (A=Z, B=Y, C=X, etc.) to find out!

WVZW   YZXGVIRZ,   WVZW   DSRGV

YOLLW   XVOOH,   ZMW   WVZW   YLWB

XVOOH   UOLZGRMT   RM   YLWB   UOFRW

How did the teen with acne leave the jail?

To get the answer to this riddle, figure out which letters are described by each fraction. Print the letters, in order, in the boxes from left to right.

1. First ⅔ of HEAVED
2. Middle ⅓ of DEBRIS
3. Last ⅗ of CHOKE
4. Last ½ of SPROUT

!

23

Nasty Rashes

Most of the time your skin is smooth, unbroken, and skin colored. But once in a while it gets itchy, oozy, bumpy, and yucky! Figure out the word and letter puzzles to find the name of six nasty rashes that can make you want to scratch your skin off!

GROSS, BUT TRUE!
"Scabies" is a nasty rash caused by a teeny tiny mite, or bug, that digs into the skin. The female mite lays her eggs, and the burrowing, growing, chomping baby mites make your skin itch like crazy. You can often see the zigzag tunnels they make as they move around. GROSS!

1. Places where bees live

2. Popular poultry + saucepan
- 20th letter + letter 3rd from end

3. Killer chemical + 9th letter
+ letter 5th from end

4. Finger jewelry + wiggly bait

5. A little stick from a needle + LY
+ 8th letter + consume food

Hurry Up!

Someone has really gotta go! Quickly collect all the words with the same number from the grid and write them in their numbered bathroom door. Rearrange the words to get the answer to each door's desperate plea.

1	4	3	2	4
Ben	the	done	will	NOW!
3	2	5	3	1
you'll	be	up	Hope	long
4	5	1	4	3
RIGHT	there!	a	toilet	soon!
1	2	3	5	2
waiting	Gwen	be	in	you
2	1	5	1	4
done?	really	Harriet	time!	Anita

1
Knock, knock.
Who's there?
Ben.
Ben who?

2
Knock, knock.
Who's there?
Gwen.
Gwen who?

3
Knock, knock.
Who's there?
Hope.
Hope who?

4
Knock, knock.
Who's there?
Anita.
Anita who?

5
Knock, knock.
Who's there?
Harriet.
Harriet who?

More Stink Pinks

The answers to Stink Pinks are two rhyming words that each have one syllable. Use the clues to figure these out!

A bunch of Boy Scouts all going #2 at the same time

_ _ _ _ _   _ _ _ _

Tiny tinkle

_ _ _   _ _ _

Long time you sat when constipated

_ _ _ _ _   _ _ _ _

Fast press of the toilet handle

_ _ _ _   _ _ _ _ _

Line of poop on the toilet paper

_ _ _ _   _ _ _ _ _

When you accidentally throw up on your mom's fancy clothes

_ _ _ _ _   _ _ _ _

What kind of nasty nuts and vulgar vegetables can you find in a toilet bowl?

Color in all the letters that appear more than three times. Read the remaining letters from left to right, and top to bottom to get the answer.

CONSTIPATION

Sometimes you just can't poop! Take this puzzle with you into the bathroom while you are waiting for "something" to happen. OK, are you sitting comfortably? Now, see how many three-letter words you can make from the letters C-O-N-S-T-I-P-A-T-I-O-N. Try to make fifteen.

Nothing yet? OK, try a little harder to make twelve words with four letters each!

Still nothing?? First, go eat some prunes. Then see if you can squeeze out five words with five letters each.

Give yourself a bonus "poop-point" for each six-letter word!

Why did the toilet paper roll down the hill?

To find out, start at the top of the hill. Pick up every other letter as you follow the roll down to the bottom of the page. The trick is to pick the correct letter to start with!

Write the correct letters on the dotted lines provided.

T T H O I G S E I T S T N O O T T H C E O B B R O R T E T C O T M

_ _

_ _ _

_ _ _

_ _ _ _ _ _!

GROSS, BUT TRUE!
On Earth, gravity makes poops plop into the toilet. But in outer space there is no gravity! That's why NASA developed a high-tech toilet that uses a vacuum to suck poop down into a special container. Otherwise, smelly "asteroids" would be floating all over the inside of the space shuttles!

Silly Sentences

Each sentence can be completed by picking one letter of the alphabet to fill in the blanks.
Can you say each sentence three times fast?

__ reddy __ arted __ ifty __ ast __ umes.

__ eter __ ooped __ artly __ ointy __ ieces.

__ ictor __ omited __ ery __ iolet __ itamins.

__ herese __ inkled __ welve __ iny __ imes.

__ illy __ lew __ lue __ oogers __ ackwards.

__ teven __ pit __ oggy __ unflower __ eeds.

GROSS, BUT TRUE! You might think that a fancy castle would have fancy bathrooms, too. Nope! The bathrooms, or "garderobes" were usually hollowed out of the wall in a tower. Some garderobes had a chute that went down into a sewer pit; others just dumped into the moat!

How do two pieces of "number 2" greet one another?

The answer to this rancid riddle has been put in a grid, and cut into pieces. Figure out where each piece fits, and fill the letters into the empty grid.

Be careful: Some of the pieces have been turned around!

Anti-Gross

While it may be fun to read about gross stuff, no one really likes to smell it.
But we all know that the air in the bathroom can get wicked gross!
Here's a recipe for a homemade air freshener that's sure to get the stink out.

You will need:
small spray bottle that holds 2-4 oz. (available at local drug store)
essential oils (available at local health food store or craft store)
bottled water, either plain or distilled
rubbing alcohol

1. To sterilize the spray bottle: Place 1 tablespoon of rubbing alcohol in the bottle, screw the lid on and shake vigorously. Dump out the alcohol and let the bottle air dry upside down. Fill the bottle with ¼ cup bottled water and add a combination of up to three different essential oils to total 15-20 drops.

2. Here are some good combinations:
   8 drops LEMON, 6 drops LAVENDER, 6 drops ROSEMARY
   5 drops CLOVE, 9 drops ORANGE, 6 drops VANILLA
   5 drops LEMON, 5 drops ORANGE, 5 drops PEPPERMINT

3. Essential oils evaporate rapidly, so don't mix batches larger than ¼ cup at a time—it will lose its scent if it sits around too long. Shake the bottle well before each use to mix the oil with the water.

GROSS AWAY SPRAY

Get rid of stink TODAY

EXTRA FUN: Make a special label for your bottle of super smell buster!

A step on a ladder	**R U N** __	
Smallest one in a litter	**R U N** __	
What a model walks down	**R U N** __ __ __	
Someone who likes to run	**R U N** __ __ __	
Breakfast and lunch combo	__ **R U N** __ __	
Past tense of drink	__ **R U N** __	
Dirty and messy	__ **R U N** __ __	
A noisy, crackling chew	__ **R U N** __ __	
A fruit that helps you poop	__ **R U N** __	
Main stem of a tree	__ **R U N** __	
Short, deep sound	__ **R U N** __	
To play again	__ __ **R U N**	

Run! Run! Run!

When you have diarrhea, you are constantly running to the bathroom. See how quickly you can complete all these words that contain the letters R-U-N.

What is white, full of poop, and can be found in a playroom?

Hold this puzzle up to the bathroom mirror and see if you can figure out how to read it!

Target Practice

Pete, Pablo, and Perry are each shooting "liquid ammunition" at this familiar target! Can you figure out who has made which puddles?

Count the points each marksman has scored using these rules:

Add the value of each ring a puddle is in

Subtract 10 points for each puddle on the bathroom floor

A direct hit in the toilet is worth 15 extra points

If a boy hasn't left any puddles on the floor, he gets 20 extra points

Pete

Pablo

Perry

20 30 40 50 40 30 20

Why did that guy . . .

To find the answer to this riddle, think of a word that best fits each of the descriptions at right. Write the words on the numbered lines, and then transfer each letter into the numbered grid.

Why did that guy bring toilet paper to a birthday party?

1D	2D	3A	4A	5C	6C	7B

8D	9E	10E		11B

12B	13E	14B	15D	16E

17C	18C	19D	20A	21A	22D

A. Robe worn by superheroes

___ ___ ___ ___
3   4   20   21

B. Autumn fruit

___ ___ ___ ___
12   7   11   14

C. Meat or veggies cooked in broth

___ ___ ___ ___
6   18   5   17

D. To annoy

___ ___ ___ ___ ___ ___
1   19   15   8   2   22

E. Not hard

___ ___ ___ ___
9   13   10   16

Gotta Go

There are many ways to say you have to go to the bathroom.
Match up the floating words to make seven different phrases.

LEAK
NATURE WHIZ
THE THE TO HEAD TAKE
CALLS CAN FILL GO
A PEE HIT A TO TAKE THE
GOT
JOHN

HINT:
Cross off words as you use them to be sure you use them all.

1. _____ _____
2. ____ __ ____
3. ___ ___ ___
4. _____ __ ____
5. ____ ____ ____
6. ___ ___ ___ ____
7. ___ ___ ___ ____

J EPO'U TXJN

JO ZPVS

UPJMFU,

TP EPO'U

QFF JO

NZ QPPM!

It's the Rule!

Figure out this letter substitution code (A=B, B=C, C=D, etc.) to find out what the lifeguard is yelling about!

Bathroom Pass

These kids all have their hands raised to go and use the bathroom. Who needs to go the most? Add all the numbers "1" and "2" hidden on each student and their desk. Whoever has the highest score gets to go first!

GROSS, BUT TRUE!
In Ancient Rome there was no toilet paper. In a public bathroom you would have to use a sponge soaked in saltwater on a stick!

The Putrid Painter

Gomer's grandpa is a famous painter, but he only uses disgusting colors! Can you figure out his favorites? The label on each tube of paint is missing letters that can be found in the word R-E-V-O-L-T-I-N-G.

S_CK
S___NNA

M___DY
G___D

S___KY
P___K

G_U_GY
G_E___

_OM____
_I_LE_

BU__P
B_U__

U_I_E
YE___OW

P_MP___
PU__P___

BA_F
B___GE

GROSS, BUT TRUE!

Hundreds of years ago, painters used to mix colored pigments with eggs to make a smooth and long-lasting paint called "egg tempera." Sometimes they would also add earwax to the mix to help get rid of tiny bubbles!

What is long and pointy and runs in a family?

Color in all the shapes that have the letters P-O-I-N-T-Y inside.

Baby Brother B.O.

One of Luis's little brothers has a load in his diaper. Using the logic clues below, can you sniff out which one it is?

He has curly hair
He is wearing a shirt and a diaper
He is sitting between Lance and Larry
He is not sucking his thumb

Lance

Luke

Leo

Larry

Lenny

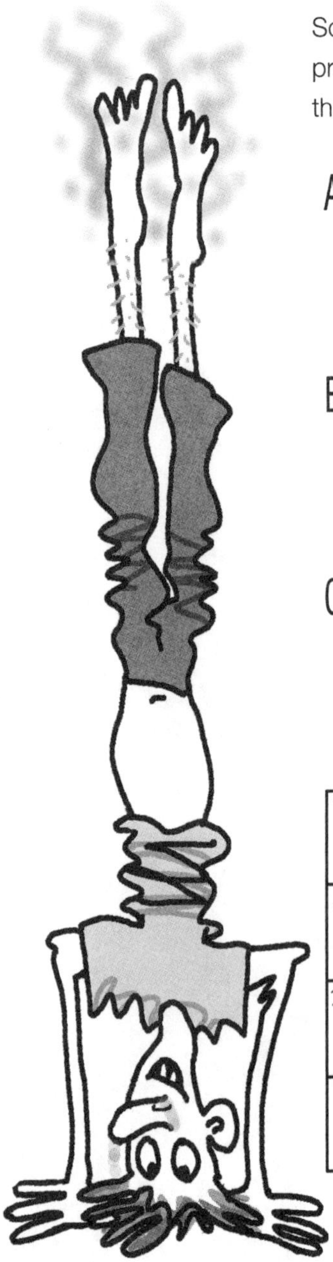

How can you tell if your brother is upside down?

Solve as many clues below as you can and put the letters in their proper place in the grid. Work back and forth between the grid and the clues until you can read the answer to this gross riddle.

A. A good time

___ ___ ___
18 9   4

B. Happy faces have these

___ ___ ___ ___ ___ ___
6 23 16 25 7 11

C. To make better

___ ___ ___ ___ ___
1 19 12 26 17

D. Number after eight

___ ___ ___ ___
10 2 13 20

E. Decays

___ ___ ___ ___
8   5 21 22

F. Small storage building

___ ___ ___ ___
3   15 24 14

1C	2D	3F		4A	5E	6B	7B
8E	9A	10D	11B		12C	13D	14F
15F	16B	17C		18A	19C	20D	21E
22E	23B	24F	25B	26C	!		

Juicy Jobs?

Some jobs just have to be done, but that doesn't mean you would want to do them! Look at the picture clues to help you unscramble each job title. Could they pay you enough to do these things?

TROPA-TOPTY NEALCER

EPT DOOF STERAT

OPOP YALSTAN

REWES VIRED

IRAMPT RFISNFE

GROSS, BUT TRUE!

The poop, pee, and everything else from 20 million people all flows into the ancient sewer system of Mexico City, Mexico. The liquid that sloshes through the more than 800 miles of pipes is so murky and full of "stuff," even a spotlight can't cut through it. That's why the special divers sent to unplug pipes and repair leaks have to feel their way around!

Uncle Leon's Lovely Leg

NOT! Uncle Leon's leg is anything but lovely. Start at his knee and see if you can find a path all the way down through his big bunion. Watch out for the varicose veins, rashes, scabs, hair, and athlete's foot along the way—eeeew!

START

END

Just Joking!

Use the names from the list, right, to answer the following questions.

Careful: There are extra names!

What would be a good name for a relative with no arms and no legs who . . .

1. ...sits in the butter dish?
2. ...sits in the mailbox?
3. ...hangs on the wall?
4. ...holds up your car?
5. ...lives in the bushes?
6. ...lies by the door?

1. _____

2. _____

3. _____

4. _____

5. _____

6. _____

PAT MATT
RUSSELL
NEAL
BILL BOB
MARK ART
JACK EILEEN

Scritch Scratch

Uncle Steve is always scratching! The names of 12 of his itchiest places are hidden in the grid below. To find them, put a different letter of the alphabet into each of the empty boxes. You might be adding the letter at the beginning, middle, or end of a word. Each letter on the list will be used only once. Circle each word as you find it.

	C	E	G	H	K	L
	M	N	O	R	S	T

1.	F	A	R		P	I	T
2.	S	C	A		P	O	P
3.	E	N	O		E	A	T
4.	B	E	L		H	I	N
5.	L	U	O		E	C	K
6.	B	A	C		S	I	D
7.	E	R	C		E	S	T
8.	O	B	U		T	E	N
9.	T	H	A		M	E	T
10.	S	L	E		I	G	E
11.	E	S	T		E	N	O
12.	R	U	B		L	L	Y

Bob's Bad Body Noises

One day Brenda counted her brother Bob making eight different disgusting noises! Can you find how many times Bob made each one? Use a light-colored marker to run a single line of color through each word you find. Make a mark in the box next to a word each time you find it.

EXTRA FUN: Use a dark marker to color all the letters X. What do you see when you're done?

BELCH
FART
GAG
GRUNT
GULP
RETCH
SNIFF
SNORT

```
W F A R T G A G W G R U N T W G
T R A F X X X X X X X K W T U
S K W X G A G B E L C H X R K L
N W X T R O N S R G A G A X W P
O X G S K X W F E K X F W T X K
R X A N X K X A T X K X W R X S
T X G I X X X R C X X X G O X N
W X F F X X X T H X X X R N X I
K X A F W F G A G W G G U S X F
S X R W A W X X X X A A N W X F
N X T R W T N U R G G G T K X B
I X T X X X X X X X X X X W X E
F X R E T C H X G G X W K T X L
F X G A G G G X A A X K R T X C
K G X W K A A X G G X O R X G H
G U W X W G G W X X N A X W A G
A L K W X G U L P S F X W K G A
G P G A G X X X X X X T R A F G
B E L C H W K P L U G S N I F F
```

Very Funny, Grandpa!

Greg's Gramps lives in a cabin without indoor plumbing. When Greg visits, he has to use the outhouse! Help him find it by making compound words through the grid. You can move left, right, up, down, but not diagonally.

START GRAND	CHILD	LIKE	WISE	MEN
MOTHER	BIRTH	DOWN	RIGHT	HORSE
HOOD	DAY	BREAK	HAND	CLOTH
ON	TIME	TABLE	OUT	HOUSE END

After visiting the outhouse, see if you can decipher this Grandpa joke.

Hint: A mirror will help!

What's the difference between Grandpa's cooking and a pile of slugs?

JUST FOLLOW YOUR NOSE...

GROSS, BUT TRUE!
Before indoor bathrooms were available, people were frequently bitten by spiders that lived in their outhouses. That's enough to make your skin crawl!

Family Photos

Can you find the 10 differences between these two photos? Which one would you send to Grandma?

What do you call your cousin who never uses a tissue to wipe his nose?

To get the answer to this joke, figure out which letters are described by each fraction. Print the letters, in order, in the boxes from left to right.

1. First 3/6 of GREASE
2. Last 1/3 of DAMPEN
3. First 1/2 of SLOP
4. Middle 1/3 of WET
5. Middle 3/5 of SEVEN
6. First 1/4 of SPIT

Relatively Gross

The next time you get together with your family, and especially a bunch of cousins your age, why not have a contest to see who can make the best gross noise? Or let everyone make a different noise, but all at the same time! Here are a few suggestions:

The Classic Armpit Fart

Put the open palm of your right hand under your left armpit. Cup the hand slightly. Now flap your left arm up and down, and squeeze the air, and fart noises, out from under your palm. This works best if your palm is moist. You can wait till you're sweaty, wet your hand in the sink, or lick your palm! You can also make fart noises by cupping your two damp hands across each other and squeezing the palms together.

Sick Elephant

You'll Need: toilet paper tube, rubber band, tape, paper punch, scissors, waxed paper

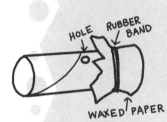

Take the tube and punch a hole in the side, about an inch from one end. Cut a circle of waxed paper bigger than the end of the tube. Use the rubber band to hold the waxed paper over the same end of tube where you punched the hole, making sure not to cover the hole. To make sick elephant sounds, put your mouth over the open end of the tube and hum, moan, sing, or talk funny.

Shriekers

Blow up a balloon and hold it closed, but not tied. Let the air out very slowly, stretching the neck of the balloon to change the sound.

Barking Belcher

You'll Need: waxed paper cup, wooden toothpick, yarn, scissors, sharp pencil

Cut a piece of yarn about 6 inches long. Soak the yarn in water until it is really wet. Tie one end around the toothpick. Use a pencil to poke a hole in the middle of the bottom of the paper cup. Push the end of the wet yarn through the hole so the yarn is hanging out of the cup and the toothpick is lying flat inside. You might have to break a bit off the toothpick to make it fit. Wet your thumb and forefinger and pinch the yarn just below the cup. Pull down hard.

HINT: If you don't get a sound, wet your fingers more. Also, a longer piece of yarn will give you a deeper belch!

What did the monster mama say to her son?

Add straight and diagonal lines to find the answer.

STOP PICKING YOUR NOSES!

EXTRA FUN: Can you tell which shadow exactly matches the picture, above?

Losing Lunch

Have a friend help you finish this story. Don't show them the story first! Ask your helper for the kind of word needed for each blank line (a description is written underneath). Write in the words your helper chooses, then read the story out loud.

EXTRA FUN: Use a pencil, then you can erase the words and try again!

(_____) I had a (_____) stomach
　　　day of the week　　　　　　　　　　awful adjective

ache. I don't know why! At lunch I only ate (_____)
　　　　　　　　　　　　　　　　　　　　　　　　big number

(_____) and (_____)(_____).
　　food item, plural　　　　　big number　　different food item, plural

For dessert I had (_____) (_____). By the time I
　　　　　　　　　　number　　　food item, plural

got home, I felt (_____). My stomach started
　　　　　　　　　　awful adjective

(_____) and my face turned (_____). I ran for the
　action word　　　　　　　　　　　　　　color

bathroom, but my (_____) brother, (_____),
　　　　　　　　　awful adjective　　　　　　　　boy's name

was in there. Sometimes he stays

in there for (_____) hours.
　　　　　　big number

Oh no! So I ran into the

(_____), instead,
room in your house, not the bathroom

and threw up in a (_____).
　　　　　　　　　　　container

I felt much better after that!

Yum! Bugs!

How would you like scorpion soup for dinner? Perhaps grasshopper tacos or spaghetti with mealworms? Believe it or not, bugs are a tasty and nutritious food! See if you can find all the edible bugs hidden in the word search.

grub
scorpion
tarantula
beetle
grasshopper
worm
termite
dragonfly
stink bug
spider
caterpillar
ant
silkworm
waterbug
cricket
cicada

```
W E Y L F N O G A R D H G
A T E K C I R C T D O Y U
O I U C I C A D A G E T B
I M F A N T B Y O U N C K
G R R T O S E S M R O W N
U E A E T E E R M I I T I
B T A R A N T U L A P G T
R E W P I T L H A B R O S
E O K I A N E I N U O S P
T E C L T T H A B T C E I
A S I L K W O R M A S T D
W S I A T S O W N W O R E
D S G R A S S H O P P E R
```

EXTRA FUN: After you have found all the bugs, collect the leftover letters from left to right and top to bottom and write them in order on the lines below.

_ _ _ _   _ _   _ _ _   _ _ _   _ _   _ _ _   _ _ _ _   _

_ _ _ _ _ _   _ _ _ _   _   _ _ _ _ ?   _ _   _ _ _ _ _ _

_ _ _ _   _ _ _ _   _ _ _   _ _ _   _ _ _ _ !

51

Waiter! There's a fly in my soup!

This man does not eat bugs. He is not pleased to find a fly in his soup! Collect all the words with the same number from the grid and write them in the numbered soup bowl. Rearrange the words to get the answers that four different waiters gave to this unhappy diner.

2 That's	3 like	2 of	3 they	1 everyone
4 has	1 quiet,	4 Oops!	2 There's	4 a
2 enough	4 Today's	3 rotten	1 will	4 yesterday's
4 soup	2 you!	1 Be	4 That's	2 for
1 want	3 Yes,	4 soup.	2 OK!	1 one!
3 food!	1 or	2 both	3 really	4 beetle.

1.

2.

3.

4.

Clean the Fridge!

Know how leftovers get when they have been in the fridge a reeeeeeally long time? Fit the eighteen words that describe how gross they look (and smell) into the grid, right. When you are done, read down the shaded column to find the answer to the riddle. We left you a few L-E-F-T-O-V-E-R-S to help!

SLIMY	**TOXIC**
STINKY	**ROTTEN**
MOLDY	**OOZING**
SCARY	**CRUSTY**
PUTRID	**SMELLY**
GREEN	**YUCKY**
RANCID	**FETID**
NASTY	**WEIRD**
FIZZY	**VOMITOUS**

What do leftovers turn into if you leave them in the fridge too long?

Peanut Butter and . . . ?

You may like peanut butter sandwiches with jelly or marshmallow. But some people like peanut butter with more unusual foods! Complete each of the food items below with letters from the word PEANUT BUTTER.

_ O L O G N _

_ O _ _ _ O CHI _ S

C H O C O L _ _ _

B _ C O _

C H _ _ S _

_ I C K L _ S

M _ S _ _ _ D

_ _ _ S L _ Y

M _ Y O _ _ _ I S _

O _ I O _

_ . _ . Q . S _ _ C _

START

END

EXTRA FUN: Munch your way through this unusual sandwich from START to END. Find any strange ingredients?

Poll your friends—which P.B. combo is their favorite?

Gag Man, Glad Man

Gag Man has to eat something slimy and gross. He will be glad when he is done! Can you help? Get through the maze alternating from Gag Man to Glad Man. You can move up and down and side to side, but not diagonally. If Gag Man throws up, you are going the wrong way!

Broccoli, Turnip, and Liver Casserole

Suppose you are served something really gross for dinner—what would you do? Ask your friends and families which of the following would be their way to deal with an awful meal (they can only pick one answer). Write their name in the square next to their choice. Your graph will show if one answer is the most popular!

Roll your eyes, but try it anyway.									
Hide it under other food on your plate.									
Slip it in your napkin to throw away later.									
Feed it to the dog.									

Lose Your Appetite

Have you ever been so grossed out watching someone eat that you just don't feel like eating your own meal anymore? While you're watching this disgusting diner, see if you can find the 15 items hidden in the mess.

Look for: cat's face, cow, key, face of a king, sock, teacup, flying bird, daisy, spoon, ghost, needle, gingerbread man, tic tac toe grid, caterpillar, witch hat.

Bug Eater

There is a special term for the practice of eating bugs. Use the clues to fill in the rows from top to bottom. When you are done, read down the shaded column.

Clue			
You sleep in this at night			
The number before two			
Past tense of eat			
Opposite of cold			
Referee at a ballgame			
Man's best friend			
Relative of a monkey			
Not "he"			
Very angry			
Years you have lived			
You wink with this			

Delicious Delicacies

A "delicacy" is something to eat that is considered rare or luxurious. Using the clues, figure out these six delicacies that some people really enjoy eating. Would you try any of them?

GROSS, BUT TRUE!

Natives of Iceland celebrate their Viking heritage at a Thorrablot feast. The menu might include sheep's blood pudding, boiled lamb's heads, and rotten shark meat—dug up after being buried for months!

Milk-giver's smart parts

_ _ _   _ _ _ _ _ _

Cud chewer's mouth muscle

_ _ _   _ _ _ _ _ _

Hopper's essential parts

_ _ _ _ _   _ _ _ _

Baa baa's tum tum

_ _ _ _ _   _ _ _ _ _ _

Ape's kissing equipment

_ _ _ _ _ _   _ _ _ _

Porker's walkers

_ _ _   _ _ _ _

make a mold factory

Molds are a kind of fungi that grow on food and in damp places. There are thousands of different kinds. Although you don't really want them in your house, molds are good natural recyclers outside. They break down foods and return nutrients to the soil. If you would like to see some molds at work, try making this "Mold Factory."

Here's what you'll need:
Permission from an adult.
1 clean, empty mayo jar with lid
Masking tape
Water
Small pieces (approx 1 inch) of food like bread, fruit, vegetables or cheese.

NOTE: Avoid meat as it will rot and smell before it grows mold.

Here's what you do:

1. Open the jar and lay it on its side.

2. Dip each piece of food in the water and place it in your container. Space the pieces so they are not all on top of each other.

3. Carefully, screw the lid on the jar and seal it with masking tape.

4. Make a label for your "Mold Factory" and attach it.

5. Put your Factory in a safe place where you can watch it.

6. Look at your Mold Factory every day. You won't see much for 2-3 days, but then molds will start to grow on the food. Answer these questions:

   What colors of mold grew?
   What texture were they?
   What food got moldy first?
   Did all the foods get moldy?

7. As the days pass, the food in your factory will start to look really gross. The mold is breaking the food down and causing it to rot.

8. Watch the changes for about two weeks. After that, not much else will happen.

9. Do not remove the lid from your Mold Factory. After two weeks, throw your factory out!

> **GROSS, BUT TRUE!**
>
> The mushrooms that many people like to eat on pizza or in spaghetti sauce are one kind of fungus. Athlete's Foot and Ringworm (both itchy, oozy skin conditions) are caused by two other kinds of fungus!

To Market

In many countries, going to the market is quite an adventure. If you were sent to get food for dinner, you might not want to eat anything! Use written and picture clues to see if you can decipher this unusual shopping list. Write the items you are shopping for in the spaces provided.

1 P.H. (with big ears)

4 D.F. (clean webbing)

3 F. (good jumpers)

4 T. (with all 8 legs)

1 S. (watch stinger)

15 W. (wiggly)

2 G. (necks 9 inches)

The Barf Buffet

What's on the menu today? Figure out which code is used for each answer. Break the codes to find out what "goodies" are being served!

1. Sore Throat Drink
2. Smells Bad Snack Food
3. Bad Hair Breakfast Food
4. Foam-at-the-Mouth Dessert

Simple Letter Shift
(A=B, B=C, C=D, etc.)

Reverse Simple Letter Shift
(A=Z, B=A, C=B, etc.)

First-to-Last Letter Shift
(BOOK becomes OOKB)

Reverse Letter Substitution
(A=Z, B=Y, C=X, etc.)

CODE WHEEL

XLFTS-VV

EBOESVGG GMZLFT

RSDMBG EQHDR

AKEC FO OAPS

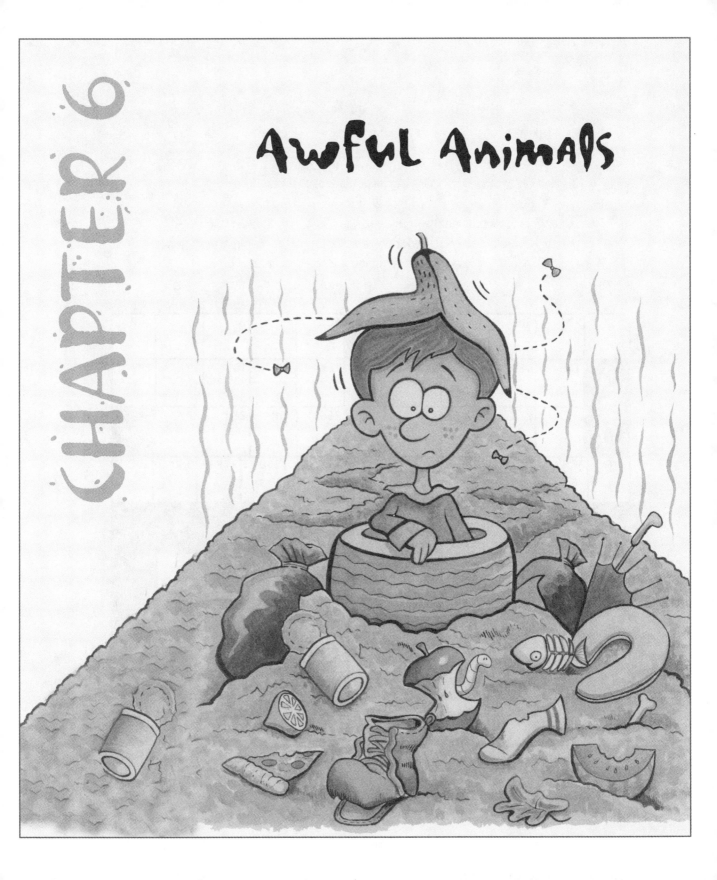

White stuff from the sky?

Remember that there are many disgusting things that can drop on you from out of the blue. Think of a word that best fits each of the clues on the next page. Write the words on the numbered lines, and then transfer each letter into the numbered grid. Work back and forth until you can read this good advice. It might just keep you from getting a whole mouthful of gross!

1Q	2M	3H	4P	5N		6C	7P	8N	9F	10D
	11H	12D	13G	14A	15L	16K	17Q	18F	19A	20J
	21D	22A	23A	24A		25Q	26H	27N	28P	
29P	30M	31Q	32G	33C	34D		35I	36Q	37R	38D	39C
	40E	41L	42M		43B	44B	45J			
46F	47I	48C	49B	50I		51K	52F	53M	54J	
55M	56L	57E	58K		59P	60L	61B	62I	63O	
64G	65R	66E		67O	68N	69K				
70R	71O	72O	73H	74H	75G	!				

A. Opposite of black

$\overline{14}$ $\overline{24}$ $\overline{22}$ $\overline{23}$ $\overline{19}$

B. A heavy, dropping sound

$\overline{43}$ $\overline{44}$ $\overline{61}$ $\overline{49}$

C. To wind around

$\overline{6}$ $\overline{33}$ $\overline{48}$ $\overline{39}$

D. High, complaining voice

$\overline{21}$ $\overline{10}$ $\overline{38}$ $\overline{12}$ $\overline{34}$

E. Past tense of run

$\overline{66}$ $\overline{40}$ $\overline{57}$

F. Opposite of front

$\overline{46}$ $\overline{52}$ $\overline{9}$ $\overline{18}$

G. Toad's relative

$\overline{64}$ $\overline{75}$ $\overline{13}$ $\overline{32}$

H. Casts a ballot

$\overline{3}$ $\overline{26}$ $\overline{73}$ $\overline{74}$ $\overline{11}$

I. Pants and jacket combo

$\overline{50}$ $\overline{35}$ $\overline{47}$ $\overline{62}$

J. Take in with the eyes

$\overline{20}$ $\overline{45}$ $\overline{54}$

K. Rear part of a foot

$\overline{51}$ $\overline{58}$ $\overline{69}$ $\overline{16}$

L. To trick

$\overline{15}$ $\overline{56}$ $\overline{60}$ $\overline{41}$

M. Winter hand covering

$\overline{55}$ $\overline{42}$ $\overline{30}$ $\overline{53}$ $\overline{2}$

N. To injure

$\overline{68}$ $\overline{27}$ $\overline{5}$ $\overline{8}$

O. Not fat

$\overline{67}$ $\overline{63}$ $\overline{71}$ $\overline{72}$

P. Look at for a long time

$\overline{59}$ $\overline{29}$ $\overline{7}$ $\overline{28}$ $\overline{4}$

Q. Live-in babysitter

$\overline{36}$ $\overline{17}$ $\overline{1}$ $\overline{31}$ $\overline{25}$

R. Number before three

$\overline{37}$ $\overline{70}$ $\overline{65}$

A Creature's Gotta Eat

It's hard to eat politely if you don't have hands to use a knife and fork. The creatures hiding in the sentences below use some pretty gross means to get a meal! Collect the capital letters in each sentence and unscramble them to see who is eating what, and how.

i Shove my StomAcH out thRough my mouth and surround what i'm eaTing. i pull It back in when i'm Full.

_____

i tHrow up On Food, and thE acid turns mY meaL to soUp. then i Slurp it up!

_____

i liVe by eating animals thaT are alReady dead. the eye-balLs are easy to get to, so it is not UnusUal that i Eat them first.

_____

i attaCh to my dinnEr's skin and suck bLood up to ninE times my weigHt.

_____

i crush an animal uNtil it stoPs breathing. then i unHook my jaws and stretch mY mouth exTra wide. this lets me swallow my dinner whOle!

_____

Some animals eat poop. Others don't. Circle YES next to the animals you think might be dung munchers. Circle NO next to those animals that aren't. Then check your answers in the back.

Rabbits	YES	NO
Cats	YES	NO
Dogs	YES	NO
Koalas	YES	NO

Those Dang Beetles

There is a small creature who is big in the gross department! To learn this critter's name, look carefully at the rings below. Some look like they are linked through each other. Others look like two rings that overlap, but are not linked. Color the linked rings and read the letters inside them from left to right and top to bottom.

To get really grossed out, break the FIRST TO LAST CODE, below, and see how this creature spends its time!

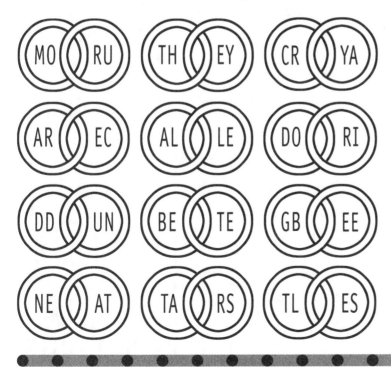

MO RU   TH EY   CR YA

AR EC   AL LE   DO RI

DD UN   BE TE   GB EE

NE AT   TA RS   TL ES

heseT eetlesb
ollectc nda
ollr allsb fo
ungd, ro
oopp, ni
hichw ot ayl
heirt ggse.
heyT lsoa ate
ungd orf
innerd!

ICK! That's what makes me sneeze?!?

Are you allergic to dust? Well, it's not actually the dust that makes you sneeze. Color in the boxes with a dot in the upper right-hand corner to learn what really gets in your nose and makes you blow! Crack the MIRROR CODE to find out more.

DAY.
HOUSE EACH
OVER THE
SHED ALL
CELLS YOU
DEAD SKIN
MILLIONS OF
EATING THE
LIVE BY
DUST MITES
MICROSCOPE.
A POWERFUL
SEE WITHOUT
SMALL TO
CRITTER TOO
IT IS A TINY
THE SPIDER.
RELATIVE OF
IS A DISTANT
A DUST MITE

Open Wide

Many snakes swallow their prey whole, and sometimes still alive! The victim slowly digests inside the snake. Can you tell what animal each of these snakes has eaten today? Choose from the list, but be careful—there are a few extra meals included!

WEASEL

FROG

BIRD

MOUSE

TOAD

WORM

RABBIT

OWL

GATOR

TURTLE

FISH

SPIDER

DEER

SNAKE

LIZARD

Nice Cow?

Picture this: a sunny day, blue sky, fluffy clouds, and a herd of peaceful cows lying in a field chewing . . . what is that stuff they're chewing anyway? Figure out the code pattern and cross out the extra words to find out!

Cows chew have chew trouble chew digesting chew the chew grass chew they chew eat chew. They chew chew chew and chew swallow chew grass chew in chew the chew field chew. Later chew, they chew upchuck chew the chew partially chew digested chew grass chew and chew rechew chew it chew — for chew up chew to chew 9 chew hours chew a chew day chew!

Shark Bite

There is a nasty species of shark that uses a suction cup mouth to clamp onto dinner as it swims by. Then it spins around, and with sawlike teeth cuts a hole in the side of the victim. After slurping the plug of flesh out of the animal, this cutter goes looking for more! Check out these sorry swimmers to find the letters that spell the descriptive name of these sharks.

C _ _ _ _ _   C _ _ _ _   S _ _ _ _ _

Big Monkeys

Fill in the letters that appear in the grid less than three times. Write the letters in order (left to right, and top to bottom) on the dotted lines to get the answer to this riddle:

What do you get when you cross big monkeys with dynamite?

B C E A F I J C D
L I L J U E F U I
C U B D L O J E O
D M F I E C F S D

_ _ - _ _ _ _ _ !

Elephant Nose Pick

Each of the letters in a column belongs in one of the boxes directly below it, but not always in the same order! After you put each letter into the correct space, you will have the answer to this riddle:

Why don't elephants pick their nose?

| T / A | B / W / H | T / E / O / H | O / E / Y / H | R / O / W | D / E / E / G | R / O / F | N / T / O / O | O / T | T / H | K / I / L | O / N / D | N / E / O | G / W |

It's Not Snot

If you live on the Pacific coast, you might find something strange in your garden. It's ten inches long, bright yellow, and covered in slime. No, it's not a living booger, but what is it?

1. Use the clues to fill in the circles. The last letter of one word is the first letter of the next. Only one letter goes in each circle. When you are done, read the shaded letters in order to learn this slimy critter's name. **HINT:** It's OK if you seem to be spelling backwards!

2. Connect the dots to get a life-sized portrait of your slippery friend! Use markers or crayons to color him yellow with a few brown spots, just like the familiar fruit it's named after. **HINT:** Use curving, not straight, lines to connect the dots.

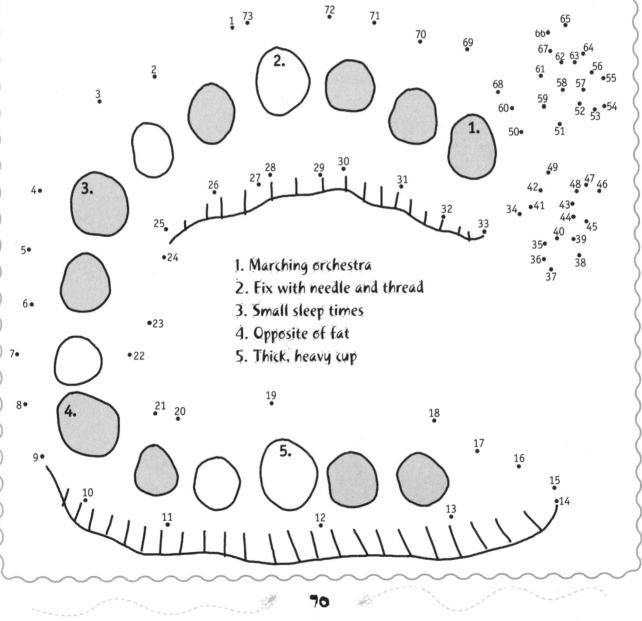

1. Marching orchestra
2. Fix with needle and thread
3. Small sleep times
4. Opposite of fat
5. Thick, heavy cup

Homemade Banana Slime

Caution: Slime is very messy, so do this activity in or near the kitchen sink!

You will need:
1 cup of cornstarch
½ cup of lukewarm water
yellow food coloring
banana extract
vegetable oil

1. Place the cornstarch into a bowl. Add one or two drops of food coloring, one or two drops of banana extract, and ¼ teaspoon of oil to the water.

2. SLOWLY pour the water mixture into the cornstarch and moosh it together with your fingers. Mix until the slime is goopy through and through.

3. Enjoy some gross and gooshy fun playing with the slime in the bowl. **EXTRA GROSS:** Carefully pour the slime into a shallow pan and add a homemade slug!

Homemade Banana Slug

Fill a thin, yellow water balloon a little less than full with water. It should not be so full that it's ready to burst. Rub your hands with a little bit of vegetable oil and grease up the "slug" before you nestle it into a pan of slime. See how it moves!

Giraffe

Break the VOWEL SCRAMBLE CODE to find the answer to this riddle:

Why do giraffes have such long necks?

BACUOSA GERUFFA FURTS SMALL SI BUD!

Slobber = ?

The human tongue is used for tasting, drinking, and making noises. A dog's tongue does these things, too. But when a dog pants on a broiling summer day, his tongue is being used to do something totally different! To find the damp and sticky answer to what a hot dog is doing, fill in the five grids using the following directions:

Fill in all the squares across the top of 1, 3, 4 and 5.
Fill in all the squares across the bottom of 1 and 3.
Fill in all the squares across the middle of 1, 3, and 4.
Fill in all the squares down the left side of 2, 3 and 4.
Fill in the squares down the right side of 2 and 4.
Fill in the squares down the center of 2 and 5.

On a hot day, a dog uses its tongue to...

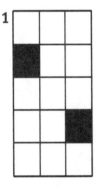
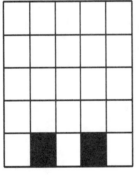
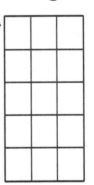

GROSS, BUT TRUE!

Jellyfish are such simple creatures that they have a digestive system with only one opening. That means they use their "mouth" for both eating and pooping!

Your breath is awful!

Sorry!

A. Not a special one

‾10 ‾11 ‾9

B. Cow noise

‾13 ‾17 ‾18

C. Opposite of work

‾19 ‾15 ‾14 ‾4

D. Center of a peach

‾16 ‾12 ‾6

E. Opposite of she

‾2 ‾3

F. Tiny bits of dirt

‾8 ‾7 ‾5 ‾1

Watch Your Step

Scatologists are scientists with a very specialized job. They study a lot of one particular thing that is found all over nature. To find out what it is, think of a word that best fits each of the clues. Write the words on the numbered lines, and then transfer each letter into the numbered grid.

What do SCATOLOGISTS do?

	1F	2E	3E	4C	
5F	6D	7F	8F	9A	
10A	11A	12D	13B	14C	15C
	16D	17B	18B	19C	

Hey, Hippo!

If two male hippos meet at the border of their territories, they have a particularly gross way of telling each other to "STAY AWAY!" What is it? Break the FIRST TO LAST Code to find out.

Hint: Hippos use their paddle-shaped tails like propellers to help spread this messy message around.

ALEM IPPOSH ILLW URNT UTTB OT UTTB NDA PRAYS ACHE THERO ITHW A LOPPYG IXTUREM FO OOPP NDA RINEU!

Feed Me

I am a plant that eats flesh. I like ants, spiders, and juicy bugs. When an insect lands in my open mouth—SNAP! I slam shut and trap the bug inside where it is slowly digested. Use a dark color to fill in the shapes that have the letters F-E-E-D M-E. The leftover white shapes will show what kind of predatory plant I am.

Yucky Yucky

The Loa loa is an African worm that likes to travel. It starts out as a tiny larvae being carried in a fly, but makes its way to someplace a lot more cozy. Follow the directions to see where it ends up.

EXTRA GROSS: As an adult, the Loa loa can grow to be over one and a half inches long!

1. Find puzzle piece 1A (on facing page) and copy it into square 1A of the grid.
2. Find piece 2A and copy it into square 2A.
3. Continue until you have copied all the puzzle pieces into the grid.
4. Crack the VOWEL SCRAMBLE CODE to read the answer across the bottom of the puzzle.

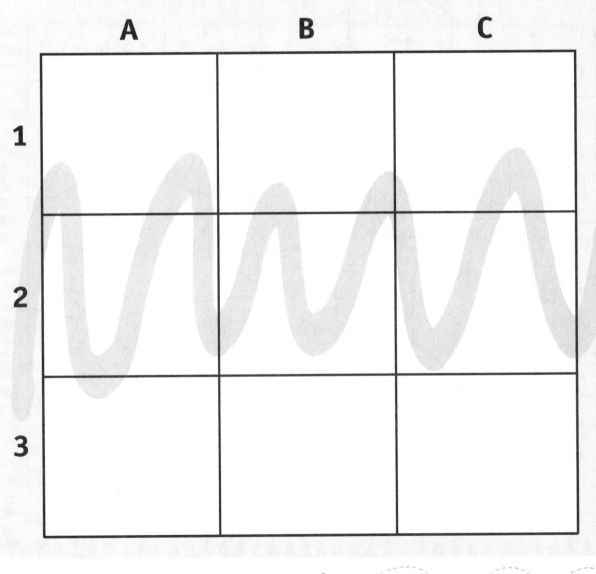

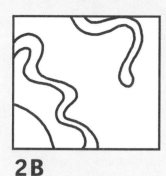

2B

3B

1B

3C

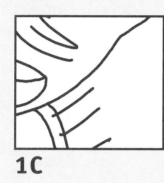

1C

3A

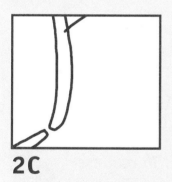

2C

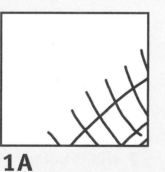

1A

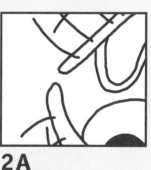

2A

Monster Eyes

Break the EXTRA LETTER Code to find the answer to this gory story:

Where did the mad scientist get eyes for his monster?

PIAIRIIISI, BIEICIAIUISIEI TIHIEI EIYIEI-FIUILILI TIOIWIEIRI IISI TIHIEIRIEI!

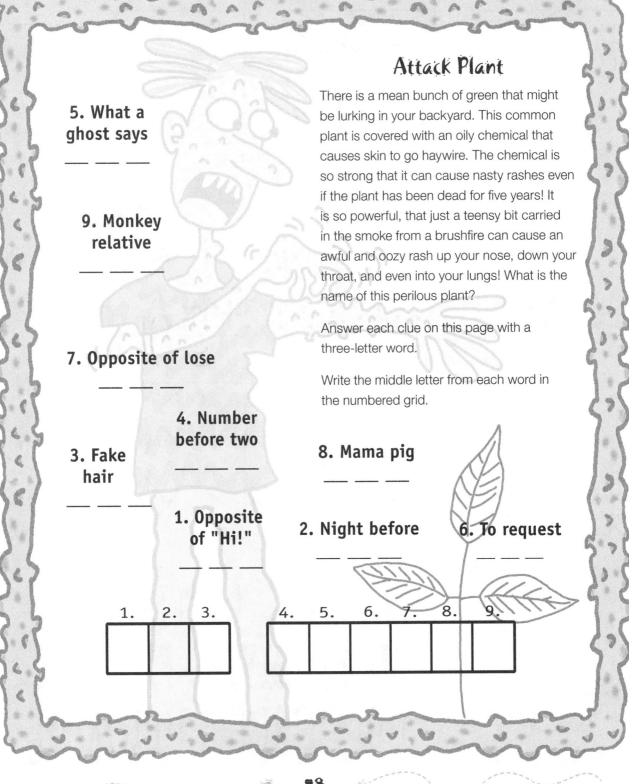

Attack Plant

There is a mean bunch of green that might be lurking in your backyard. This common plant is covered with an oily chemical that causes skin to go haywire. The chemical is so strong that it can cause nasty rashes even if the plant has been dead for five years! It is so powerful, that just a teensy bit carried in the smoke from a brushfire can cause an awful and oozy rash up your nose, down your throat, and even into your lungs! What is the name of this perilous plant?

Answer each clue on this page with a three-letter word.

Write the middle letter from each word in the numbered grid.

5. What a ghost says

— — —

9. Monkey relative

— — —

7. Opposite of lose

— — —

3. Fake hair

— — —

4. Number before two

— — —

8. Mama pig

— — —

1. Opposite of "Hi!"

— — —

2. Night before

— — —

6. To request

— — —

1.	2.	3.		4.	5.	6.	7.	8.	9.

Smelly Letters

What are the four smelliest letters in the alphabet?

Color in the letters that appear only one time. Then read the dark letters from left to right and top to bottom to get the answer!

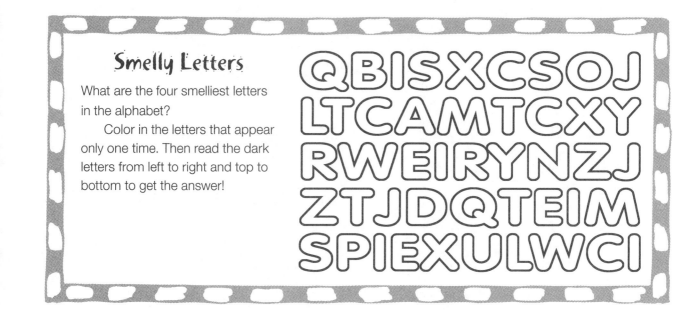

QBISXCSOJ
LTCAMTCXY
RWEIRYNZJ
ZTJDQTEIM
SPIEXULWCI

How Many Farts

See if you can find the nine letters that make up the answer to this riddle. Write them in the correct order on the dotted lines.

How many farts does it take to fill a school bus? _ _ _ _ _ _ _ _ _ !

Where's the Gross?

Can you underline the eight gross words hiding in these sentences? The words you're looking for are in the list, but careful — there are a few extras!

soiled   retch
rotten   spit
gore   snot
scab   nasty
foul   gag
slime   grimy
gross   slug

1. The kids lugged four cans of garbage.
2. The slim earthworm poops in the dirt.
3. While belching, Ross can also chant.
4. Joe's pit bull was chewing a greasy bone.
5. The secret chain opens the dirty drain.
6. Does anyone eat warthog or electric eel?
7. Bob's note was dumb and disgusting.

That's great!

Why was the pig farmer thankful when a bird pooped on his head?

Use the directions to cross out words in the grid. Read the remaining words and you will get the answer. Cross out all words . . .

. . . that rhyme with PEE and have three letters
. . . that end in NK
. . . that start with FO

HE	FOE	WAS	THINK
TANK	THANKFUL	SEA	FOG
THAT	FORGETFUL	PIGS	RANK
TEA	CAN'T	FEE	FLY

Sloppy Sentences

Add one letter to each of the blanks in the sentences to the right. Each sentence will use a different letter.

_even _limy _lugs _lid _oftly _ideways.

_ary's _reasy _uts _rew _reen _arbage.

_ig _lack _ugs _leed _lack _lood.

_oul _eces _lopped _rom _ive _latworms.

_any _aggots _ake _oist _eals _essy.

B-U-T-T Spells . . .

Play this game in teams like charades, but instead of trying to mime or spell a word out with your hands, face, or body language, use your rear end to spell out the word! The first team to shout out the correct word wins the point.

Scaggy Scavenger Hunt

How many gross things can you find lurking in your house? Keep a copy of the list below for yourself, and make a copy for a sibling or parent. Then search your house from top to bottom. Each item is worth 3 points. Whoever gets the most gross points wins!

___ **pet poop**
___ **hairball**
___ **dust bunny**
___ **smelly sock**
___ **sour milk**
___ **toenail clipping**
___ **used cotton swab**
___ **used bandage**
___ **moldy leftover**
___ **dried booger**
___ **chewed gum**
___ **dead insect**
___ **other** _____

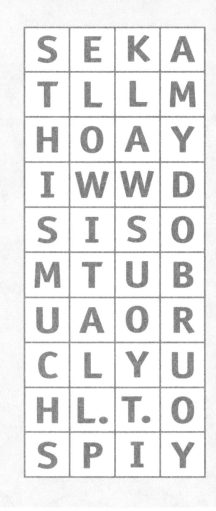

Here's a few rules:

Don't pick up the gross stuff you find. Just check it off your list and add up the points.

If you want to play with a friend, let him search his house while you search your own house. Get together later to compare results.

Gross Gulps

Your body makes between four and six cups of this stuff each day. You get rid of most of it without a thought. What is it? Where does it go? The answer is hidden in the letter grid. Start in one of the four corners, and read the letters in a logical order. You have to figure out in which direction to read!

S	E	K	A
T	L	L	M
H	O	A	Y
I	W	W	D
S	I	S	O
M	T	U	B
U	A	O	R
C	L	Y	U
H	L.	T.	O
S	P	I	Y

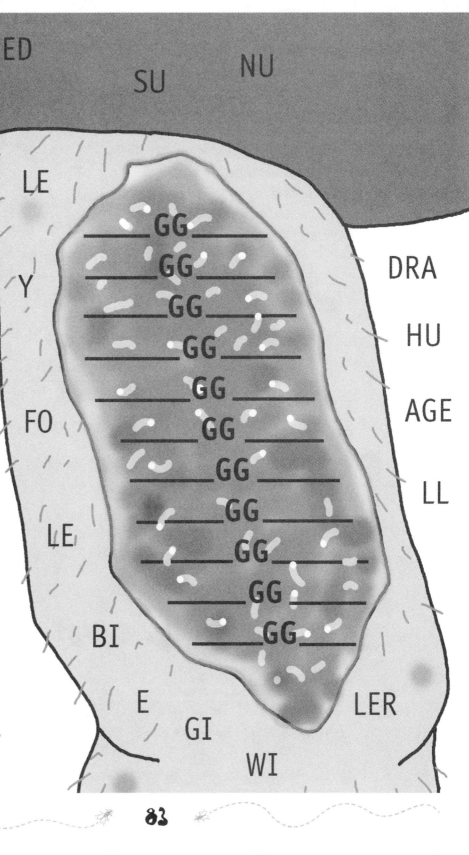

ET

ED

SU

NU

JU

ER

LE

RO

BA

DRA

ED

Y

EST

HU

FO

AGE

GG
_____ GG _____
_____ GG _____
_____ GG _____
GG _____
_____ GG _____
_____ GG _____
_____ GG _____
_____ GG _____
_____ GG _____
_____ GG _____

LL

LE

BI

E

LER

GI

WI

Got Maggots?

The larvae of a Blowfly can be placed in a deep wound where they eat dead tissue and kill harmful bacteria. The maggots in this wound have eaten away all the letters except for the GGs. Use the letters and letter pairs scattered around the page to fix the words.

HINT: Some letters make sense in more than one word, but there is only one way that uses all the letters.

Terribly Tiny

A mite is a teensy, tiny creature related to a spider. Even though you have never seen them, there are bunches of mites living very close to you. Up to 25 mites at a time can cram themselves head-first into this very small space. They eat during the day, and at night wiggle out to mate and lay their eggs. Use the decoder to learn where these common mites like to hide. Be careful—do you really want to know?

Where are they?!

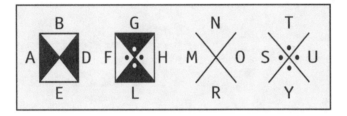

Ouch!

In 1848, Phineas Gage had an awful accident with the iron "tamping rod" he used to set explosive charges. The blasting powder Phineas was working with went off too soon, and there was no time to get out of the way. Doctors were amazed that after the accident Phineas could walk, talk, and make jokes! Even though Phineas recovered, his personality changed quite a bit. Why do you think that might be? Connect the numbered dots to show a picture of Phineas, and you will see why!

CAREFUL: There are two different sets of numbers for the dots! One set is regular (1-35), and the second set is underlined (1-38).

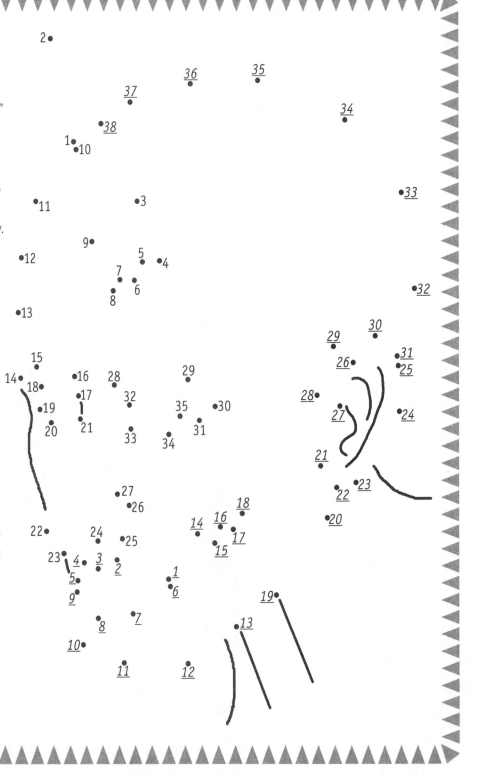

Awfully Ancient

For more than 3,000 years humanity has been plagued by an infectious disease called "leprosy" which attacks the nerves of the hands, feet, and face. Doctors only found a way to treat it about 50 years ago. However, if left untreated, leprosy can have some awful results!

In each row, cross out the letters that appear more than three times. The remaining letters will spell out the answers.

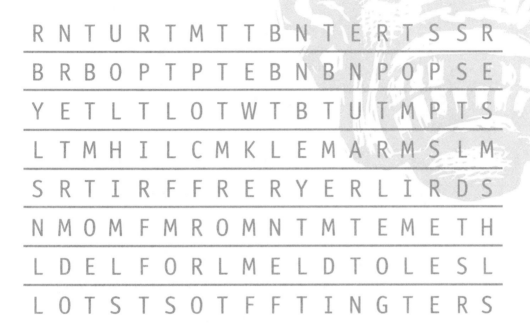

R N T U R T M T T B N T E R T S S R

B R B O P T P T E B N B N P O P S E

Y E T L T L O T W T B T U T M P T S

L T M H I L C M K L E M A R M S L M

S R T I R F F R E R Y E R L I R D S

N M O M F M R O M N T M T E M E T H

L D E L F O R L M E L D T O L E S L

L O T S T S O T F F T I N G T E R S

Nail Biter

Use this hint to break the coded answer.

Flip Flop

Doctor, Doctor! How can I stop biting my nails?

MEAR YOUR SHOES!

Seriously Surgical

The *Guinness Book of World Records* lists a man who has had the most operations ever! Most of the surgeries were to remove tumors on his face. To see how many operations he's had, fill in each blank with a number from the clue. Then add them up. Be ready for a BIG answer!

A decade is ? years ____
Cards in a deck ____
A score is ? years ____
Twelve pairs of shoes ____
Fingers on two hands ____
A gross equals ? items ____
Eighty quarters is ? dollars ____
An egg carton holds ? eggs ____
Two cups of butter is ? sticks ____
There are ? days in a year ____
There are ? keys on the piano ____
Number of pennies in a dollar ____
Ten gallons of milk is ? quarts ____
An octogenarian is ? years old ____
Number of pits in an avocado ____

TOTAL ____

Awful Smell

Use this hint to break the coded answer:

Picture Words

Doctor, Doctor! I want something to make my awful smell go away!

  !

Almost Everybody Gets It

A huge number of people use creams, powders, and sprays to treat this skin infection. In fact, about 70% of the world's population will get this infection at least once in their life! To find out what it is, figure out a word that fits each description below. Write it on the dotted lines. Then, read the circled letters from top to bottom.

If you are under 12, you probably have not had your first case of this skin infection!

A little hot = _ _ _ _

Foot digit = _ _ _

Stand-up bath = _ _ _ _ _ _

Body dryer = _ _ _ _ _ _

Opposite of dry = _ _ _ _

Scratch this = _ _ _ _

To perspire = _ _ _ _ _

Foot bottom = _ _ _ _

No foot cover = _ _ _ _ _ _ _ _

Soft foot cover = _ _ _ _ _

Hard foot cover = _ _ _ _ _

Barely wet = _ _ _ _ _

Had it?	
yes	no

Poll your grown-up family and friends.

What percentage have had this infection before?

Swallowed Pen

Use this hint to break the coded answer:

B=C
C=B

Doctor, Doctor! I swallowed a pen! What should I do?

VTF B QFODJM UJM J HFU UIFSF!

Sticky Solution

Acupuncture is a healing art that has been used in China for thousands of years. It is hard to imagine that this treatment makes you feel better, but it can! What does an acupuncturist do? Cross out words using the following rules. The remaining words are the answer.

CROSS OUT words that . . .

. . . are two letters and start with an A

. . . have a U in the exact middle

. . . end in a vowel

BODY
BODE
BUD
ARE
YOUR
ACE
BE
BUS
OVER
RUM
ALE
ALL
AS
SKUNK
STICK
AN
LOUNGE
LONG
AT
LOVE
THIN
THINE
AN
APE
NEEDLES
NOODLE
TUNE
IN
PUN
PANE
DUDE
YOUR
SCONE
SKIN

Run Down

Use this hint to break the coded answer:

First to Last

Doctor, Doctor! What should I take if I feel run down?

heT icensel latep umbern
fo het arc hatt ith ouy!

90

Rhinowhat?

There are complicated medical words to describe the most common, and gross, things! To figure out what Doctor Doofus is talking about, first unscramble each definition. Then draw a line to match it to the correct medical term.

look deep the a inside nose close

and yellow the nose of from flow liquid green

picking nose constant

GROSS, BUT TRUE!

"Rhinorrhea" shares a word-part with a common ailment that causes you to run to the bathroom in a hurry. Can you think of this other word? How would you like that coming out your nose??

You must stop that **RHINOTILLEXOMANIA** while I do a **RHINOSCOPY** to look more closely at your **RHINORRHEA**!

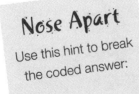

Nose Apart

Use this hint to break the coded answer:

AEIOU

Doctor, Doctor! Why did you take the patient's nose apart?

_ W _ NT _ D T _ S _ _

WH _ T M _ D _ _T R _ N!

Body Sculpting

Some people will do anything to get a slimmer body. Doctors use a procedure called LIPOSUCTION to help these people, but you won't believe what it is! Write letters from the puzzle pieces in the correct spaces of the grid to find out.

Brain Surgeon

Use this hint to break the coded answer:

A=1
Z=26

Doctor, Doctor! How did you become a brain surgeon?

9   23-1-19   1   4-5-14-20-9-19-20

21-14-20-9-12   13-25

4-18-9-12-12   19-12-9-16-16-5-4!

Slimy Helpers

A doctor who is trying to reattach a finger or an ear onto an accident victim needs all the help he can get. It is very important to get fresh blood flowing through the part that is being sewn back on. Doctors have started to use a little "helper" that was popular as long as 2,000 years ago. While this pump is beautifully designed by nature to keep blood moving, it sure isn't pretty to look at. In fact, it's downright disgusting! Fill in the shapes that contain the letters B-L-O-O-D S-U-C-K-E-R to find out what doctors might stick on a newly attached body part.

Doctor, Doctor! How can I stop catching diseases caused by biting insects?

STOP BEING MEAN!

Where does Mrs. Doctor keep spare body parts?

To find the answer to this riddle, think of a word that best fits each of the clues. Write the words on the numbered lines, and then transfer each letter into the numbered grid.

1F	2F	3B		4A	5C	6F	7A	8F		
9E	10B	11A	12D		13E	14B		15E	16A	17C
18D	19C	20E	21F	22C	23D	24C	!			

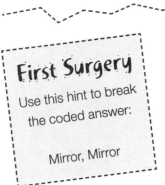

A. To continue to have

___ ___ ___ ___
4 11 16 7

B. A female chicken

___ ___ ___
10 3 14

C. Boat with a flat bottom

___ ___ ___ ___ ___
22 19 17 24 5

D. Meat from a pig

___ ___ ___
18 23 12

E. Opposite of fat

___ ___ ___ ___
9 15 13 20

F. Small storage buildings

___ ___ ___ ___ ___
8 2 6 21 1

First Surgery
Use this hint to break the coded answer:

Mirror, Mirror

Doctor, Doctor! I'm scared! This is the first time I've had surgery!

Surgeon: I know just how you feel. This is the first time I've done any!

94

"I don't feel very good . . ."

What's making you feel so gross? The doctor has left a few possibilities, and a few germs, in the puzzle grid. Now you have to figure out a word or two that fits each description below. Write them in the grid, too.

ACROSS

4. Feel sleepy
5. Stomach eruption
8. Hacking sound
9. Pain in the guts
11. Nasal flood
14. Hard to breathe
16. Burning and shivering

DOWN

1. Swallowed sandpaper
3. Runny poop
10. Pain in the skull
12. Nose blow up

GROSS, BUT TRUE!

Be careful if you have a stomach-ache or diarrhea while traveling through certain places in China. A popular remedy is a strong tea brewed out of "frass," otherwise known as caterpillar poop!

Double Vision

Use this hint to break the coded answer:

Sounds Like

Doctor, Doctor! Can you fix my double vision?

Ee her vee shun iz phu eye n. Thuh purr ah blem eez yoo haa vuh tew heh duz!

Really Rotten

Doctors never like to see this condition, because it means that part of their patient has started to rot! The body part that's in trouble turns black, and the smell can be awful. To find out what this creepy condition is called, use the clues to fill in the blanks. The last letter of one word is the first letter of the next. When you are done, write the numbered letters in the spaces provided.

1. A pet ____ pig
2. End of a prayer
3. Xmas Spice
4. Male goose

5. To lift up
6. Opposite of odd
7. Letter after eight
8. Not difficult

1	2	3	4	5	6	7	8

Headache

Use this hint to break the coded answer:

Vowel Mix

Doctor, Doctor! Can you cure this terrible headache?

Yas! Crush yior haud thriogh thut wendiw und tha puna well ba gina!

Zombie Newspaper Article

Break the REVERSE WORD
Code to read the latest news.

THE DAILY POOP

TOILET
NEWS
PAPER

EIBMOZ SESOL NOHTARAM YB EDIW NIGRAM

retfA etiuq a ylevil trats, eibmoz etelhta, retseF .N ttoR, saw deyamsid ot hsinif eht ecar daed tsal.

What's the last thing to go through a bug's mind as he hits a car windshield?

Collect the letters along the path from START to END.

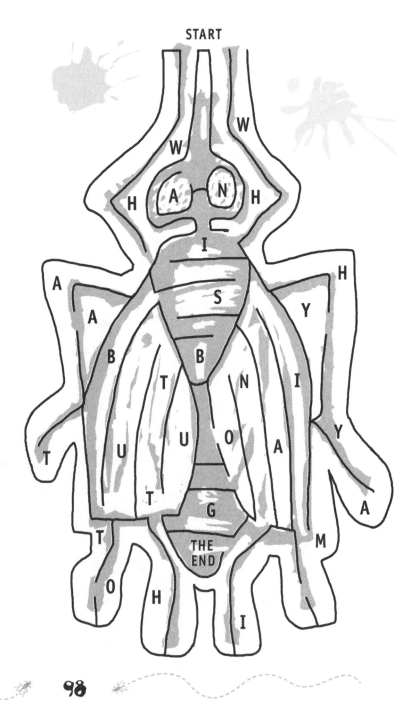

From the fourteenth to the seventeenth century there was a medicine popular in Europe called "mummy." It was made from—you guessed it—ground-up mummies. When the supply of real mummies ran low, untrustworthy medicine makers used any old, dried out bodies they could find. Or make.

Dead on My Feet

These two zombies are both out for a midnight stroll. At first glance, they look gruesomely the same. Can you find the 13 differences between these two pictures?

Cannibal King Newspaper Article

Break the AEIOU/12345
Code to read the latest news.

THE DAILY POOP

TOILET
NEWS
PAPER

44PS!

Th3s r2p4rt
j5st 3n fr4m
L41 L41 3sl1nd.
3nf1m45s
C1nn3b1l K3ng,
W1nn1 21tch1,
1cc3d2nt1lly
p5t h3s f1ls2
t22th 3n
b1ckw1rds 1nd
1t2 h3ms2lf.

Chop Chop

What is a guillotine (gill-uh-teen)? It is a very tall cutting machine with a heavy blade that drops down between two posts. It was designed a long time ago for just one awful purpose. Add straight lines to see what.

To find out what else a guillotine is, copy the pattern in each numbered square into the empty grid.

ZOMBIE HEADS

You will need:
several apples, with stems
vegetable peeler
small metal teaspoon
variety of dried materials for making features
    (such as twine, cloves, dried beans, rice,
    dried corn kernels, pasta, etc.)
wooden skewer
string

1. Peel the apples. Leave the stems in!

2. With the blunt end of the peeler or the metal teaspoon, carefully gouge out eyes, nose, mouth, and ears into each peeled apple. The carving doesn't have to be perfect. Also, since the apple will shrink a lot, making features bigger and thicker is better.

2. Poke beads, rice, beans, etc., into the apple to make eyes and teeth. Black-eyed peas or cloves make especially good eyes. Raw rice, dried corn, or broken noodles make good teeth.

3. Knot the end of the string around the stem. Hang the apple in a warm and dry place. Make sure the apple is not touching anything. Or, you can set the heads on a metal cookie cooling rack out of the sun.

4. Visit your zombie heads every few days. When the apples begin to turn leathery, you can change their expressions by pinching and twisting the features. In a few weeks you'll have some amazing shrunken faces. YUCK!

Batman Newspaper Article

Break the FIRST TO LAST Code to read the latest news.

THE DAILY POOP

TOILET
NEWS
PAPER

YNAMICD UOD ITH YB TEAMS OLLERR

atmanB nda obinR rea xpectede ot ecoverr, utb ska hatt het ublicp own eferr ot hemt sa "latmanF nda ibbonR."

Dead Poet's Society

Can you dig the rotten rhyme out of the cemetery? To find it, color in the following kinds of words, and read the remains from top to bottom, left to right. You must put the punctuation in the correct places.

SHOES
ODD NUMBERS
GROSS BODY STUFF
BODY PARTS WITH FOUR LETTERS

SEVEN SNEAKER DEAD
VOMIT MAN ON THE
BRIDGE ONE LAST
NIGHT POOP HIS CLOG
BONES WERE THREE
ALL EARWAX AQUIVER
HE SPIT GAVE A FART
COUGH HIS BOOT LEG
FOOT FELL YUCK OFF
SANDAL AND FLOATED
FIVE DOWN POOP THE
BUTT HEAD RIVER

I tightly wrapped

H body cavity is stuffed with

given a salt bath

A

Mummy Mia!

Mummies look pretty cool, but do you know what happened to those bodies before they were all neatly boxed in a sarcophagus? It is not pretty! Finish each sentence by choosing one phrase from the edge of the page. Write the letter from the phrase on the empty line. When you're finished, you'll know how ancient Egyptians preserved their mummies (and their daddies, too!)

G

are removed and put in jars

B

1. Body is _____ on the left side.

2. Lungs, liver, stomach, and intestine_____.

3. The brain is _____.

4. The heart is the only organ _____.

5. The inside of the body is _____.

6. Body is_____ and left to dry for two months.

7. Body is_____ that comes from trees.

8. _____ sand, sawdust, and cloth.

9. Body is_____ in linen bandages.

painted with resin

F

cleaned with wine

C

left in the body

cut open **D**

E pulled out through the nose

Karate Newspaper Article

Break the EXTRA WORD Code
to read the latest news.

THE DAILY POOP
TOILET
NEWS
PAPER

**KAROUCHATE
EXPOUCHERT
KNOOUCHCKED
OOUCHUT
FIROUCHST
DAOUCHY
IOUCHN
AROUCHMY**

Priouchvate
Bouch. Beouchlt
wouchas
practouchicing
hoouchw toucho
salouchute.

Hangman's Holiday

Can you match the following riddles with their answer?
Write the correct number in front of each picture puzzle.

1. **What do hangmen like to read?**
2. **Where do hangmen like to swim?**
3. **What's a hangman's favorite fruit?**

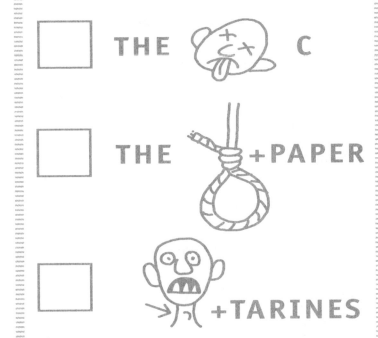

GROSS, BUT TRUE!

Beck Weathers was left for dead during a terrible
blizzard on Mt. Everest. He survived the storm,
but lost his nose to frostbite. Doctors made him
a new nose out of cartilage from his ears and
ribs. They created the nose upside-down on
Beck's forehead, using a flap of skin with healthy
blood vessels. When the nose was "finished,"
they flipped it around to the proper place.

Hangman

It's pretty gross to think that this fun and familiar game is really based on a gruesome form of execution! So to make sure no one accidentally gets "stretched," get rid of all the ropes, and grab a pencil and piece of paper instead.

To play:

1. Find a partner to play with you. One of you will think up the word (the drawer) and the other will try to guess it (the guesser).
2. The drawer thinks up a word and tells the guesser how many letters it has.
3. The guesser guesses one letter at a time. If the letter is in the word, the drawer writes it in the proper space or spaces. If not, the drawer writes the used letter next to the gallows and draws the head on the hangman.
4. Play continues and a new body part is (head, stick body, arms, legs, eyes, nose, frown) added to the hangman each time a wrong letter is guessed.

TO WIN: Either the guesser or the drawer can win. If the guesser figures out the word before the hangman is completely drawn, then he wins. But if he doesn't, then the drawer wins. The guesser can also try to solve the word at any time, but automatically loses the game if he or she is wrong.

Example

The guesser in this game did not guess the word "slippery" before the hangman was completely drawn. The guesser loses. Too bad!

GALLOWS

F O U
M T A
H C B
G

_ L I _ _ E R _

Try playing this game with only gross words! Here's a list:

STINKY

OOZING

CRUSTY

MOLDY

PUTRID

ROTTEN

REPULSIVE

HORRIBLE

DECAYING

CREEPING

SKELETAL

HIDEOUS

Indian Chief Newspaper Article

Break the ALL MIXED UP Code to read the latest news.

THE DAILY POOP
TOILET
NEWS
PAPER

INDIAN CHIEF DIES IN STRANGE ACCIDENT

Chief Hot Mug reportedly drank fifteen cups of tea before going to bed last night. He was found this morning, drowned in his own tee-pee.

What does the headstone say for the man who struck a match by the leaky gas tank?

Collect the letters blown around and write them in the correct order on these lines. We left some hints.

H _   R _ _ _ _ _
I _   P _ _ _ _ _

Can you put the scattered scatterbrain back together? Circle the four pieces that make a whole man. We left you a "before" picture!

Break the VOWEL SCRAMBLE Code
to read the latest news.

THE DAILY POOP

TOILET
NEWS
PAPER

MUD SCEANTEST TORNS ENTI FRIG

Dictir Graanbliid's mithar wus qoitad us suyeng "E tild hem navar ti leck tha spiin uftar mexeng u naw pitein!"

Dead End

A dead end means there is nowhere else to go. You are finished! You must stop! Our final puzzle in this book is to figure out all these words that contain the word E-N-D. Use the letters and letter pairs scattered around the page. Each one is used only once. Goodbye, gross friENDs!

SS

LE

PR

B

SP

S

L

FRI

REC

OFF

ER

BL

OMM

ABLE

ET

Rotten bananas are very _ E N D _ _ _ _.

Would you really eat a bug, or just _ _ _ _ E N D to?

A true _ _ _ E N D will _ E N D you his whoopie cushion.

Would you _ _ E N D your money on garlic gum or earwax candy?

A boring monster movie seems E N D _ _ _ _.

A really gross joke might _ _ _ E N D your grandma.

Some things should not go in a _ _ E N D _ _.

The gross cook _ _ _ _ _ _ E N D _ the scorpion soup.

Appendix 1
Look Again!

Just when you thought the gross was all gone, there's more! See if you can find each of these picture pieces somewhere in this book. Write the name of the puzzle each piece is from in the space under each box. **HINT:** There is only one picture piece from each chapter.

1.

2.

3.

4.

5.

6.

7.

8.

9.

References

If you haven't had enough of gross stuff, there are plenty of books you can read or Web sites you can visit. Below are listed a few of our favorites.

Books

Oh Yuck! The Encyclopedia of Everything Nasty
By Joy Masoff (2000). If you want to know "all the best stuff about some of the worst stuff on earth," then this is the book for you. From acne to eye gunk, fleas to feet, parasites to puking, it is all here.

Gross Universe: Your Guide to All Disgusting Things Under the Sun
By Jeff Szpirglas (2004). A guide to many of the disgusting, yet amazing, things in our world—be it animal, plant—or human.

Phineas Gage: a Gruesome But True Story About Brain Science
By John Fleischman (2002). The fascinatingly true story about how one man's horrible accident has helped doctors understand the workings of the human brain.

Grossology series (1995–2004)
By Sylvia Branzei. A best-selling book series including the titles *Grossology and You, Animal Grossology, Hands-On Grossology* and others. Lots of information on all things gross and disgusting, combined with hands-on activities.

Nature's Yucky
By Lee Ann Landstrom (2003). Explores icky, but interesting, facts about the behavior of some animals—and the good reasons they have for what they do.

Revolting Recipes (1997);
Even More Revolting Recipes (2001)
By Roald Dahl. Based on foods from his famous children's books, these fun, simple recipes sound worse than they really are. Anyone for a stink bug egg?

Web Sites

www.guinnessworldrecords.com
Get lost here looking at the world records for strange diseases, incredible body parts and medical marvels. Whether it is the champion eyeball-popper, the longest sneezing bout, or the person-who-can-spit-a dead-cricket-the-farthest, we guarantee you will be fascinated!

http://yucky.kids.discovery.com
This site declares itself the "Yuckiest Site on the Internet"! It contains lots of information on gross and cool body stuff, and has whole sections on worms and roaches. It also has a great fun and games area that is divided into things like creepy crafts, revolting recipes, and icky experiments.

www.grossology.org
The Web site of Sylvia Branzei and Jack Keely, author and illustrator of the Grossology series (see books to the left). Information on both individuals, a grossology store, and recipes for fake blood, barf, snot—and more!

PUZZLE ANSWERS

page v • Vowel Scramble

Knock, Knock.
Who's there?
Watson.
Watson who?
Watson your nose? It looks like a big old booger!!

page 2 • What do you get . . .

A. Says "BOO"
G H O S T
42 47 48 1 50

B. To cast a ballot
V O T E
44 49 5 4

C. A small clue
H I N T
22 23 31 41

D. To push hard
S H O V E
19 25 37 29 27

E. Opposite of fat
T H I N
10 6 43 40

F. To put up a picture
H A N G
11 12 17 24

G. A precious jewel
G E M
9 30 3

H. Cousin of a frog
T O A D
13 2 46 35

I. Bugs at a picnic
A N T S
28 8 15 14

J. Do, Re, or Me
N O T E
34 21 20 45

K. Past tense of SAY
S A I D
32 33 7 36

L. Long walks
H I K E S
26 16 18 38 39

1A S	2H O	3G M	4B E	5B T	6E H	7K I	8I N	9G G
10E T	11F H	12F A	13H T		14I S	15I T	16L I	17F N	18L K	19E S
	20J T	21J O		22C H	23C I	24F G	25D H	
26L H	27D E	28I A	29D V	30G E	31C N	32K S		33K A	34J N	35H D
	36K D	37D O	38L E	39L S	40E N		41C ' T	
42A G	43E I	44B V	45J E		46H A		47A H	48A O	49B O	50A T

SOMETHING THAT STINKS TO HIGH HEAVENS AND DOESN'T GIVE A HOOT

page 3 • Pillow P.U.

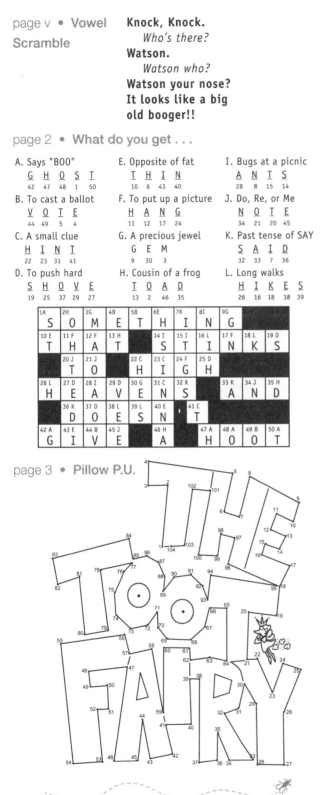

page 4 • What did the mad scientist say . . .

(crossword grid)

YOU REEK-A! (EUREKA!)

page 5 • Officially Bad Breath

LIHIC	C H I L I
STIVACIE	C A V I T I E S
QUELAP	P L A Q U E
CLIRAG	G A R L I C
RATRAT	T A R T A R
FEEFOC	C O F F E E
SNIOON	O N I O N S
FINSECTION	I N F E C T I O N S
MOGINKS	S M O K I N G

page 5 • Do What?

BRUSH YOUR TONGUE

PUZZLE ANSWERS

page 6 • Fart Foods

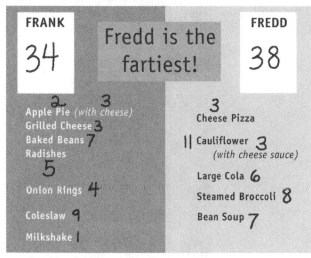

FRANK 34

Fredd is the fartiest!

FREDD 38

Apple Pie *(with cheese)* 2
Grilled Cheese 3
Baked Beans 7
Radishes 5
Onion Rings 4
Coleslaw 9
Milkshake 1

Cheese Pizza 3
Cauliflower 3 *(with cheese sauce)*
Large Cola 6
Steamed Broccoli 8
Bean Soup 7

page 8 • Stink Pinks

An intelligent toot
S M A R T   F A R T

Seven days of smelliness
R E E K   W E E K

A fish fart
B A S S   G A S

A hard, quick sniff
S T I F F   W H I F F

Smell from a moldy camping shelter
T E N T   S C E N T

An apple passing gas
F R U I T   T O O T

Smelly odor from a liquid you might swallow
D R I N K   S T I N K

page 8 • Disgusting Dump

five cartons of sour milk

page 9 • Funky Fertilizer

WHAT ARE YOU DOING WITH ALL THAT MANURE?

I'M PUTTING IT ON MY CORN.

YUCK! I PUT BUTTER AND SALT ON MINE!

page 10 • Smelling Sweet?

SWEET	tastes like sugar
SWEAT	salty body fluid
SWEAR	to say curse words
SPEAR	sharp, pointy weapon
SPEAK	to utter words
SPANK	to slap on the butt
STANK	past tense of stink
STALK	main stem of a plant
STALL	horse's room in a barn
SHALL	formal form of "will"
SHELL	hard outer covering
SMELL	to use your nose

page 10 • Smell vs. Smell

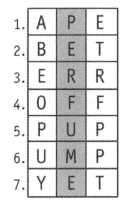

1. A P E
2. B E T
3. E R R
4. O F F
5. P U P
6. U M P
7. Y E T

page 11 • Super Sweat

PUZZLE ANSWERS

page 11 • It Was the Dog!

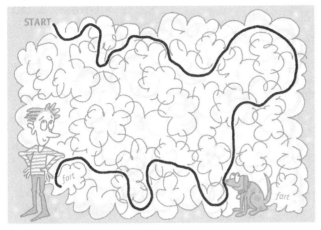

page 15 • X-tremely Gross

page 12 • Ode to Odor

<u>Black</u> socks, they never get <u>dirty</u>.

The <u>longer</u> you <u>wear</u> them,

the <u>blacker</u> they get!

<u>Night</u> falls, you <u>dream</u>

of the <u>laundry</u>, but

<u>something</u> inside you

says, "Don't <u>wash</u> them yet!"

page 16 • Slop Talk

1. **S P I T**
2. **F L I T**
3. **K N I T**
4. **Q U I T**
5. **G R I T**

page 16 • Ah-Zoom!

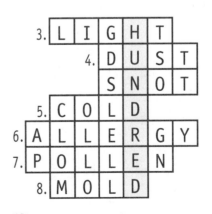

page 12 • Stinky Socks

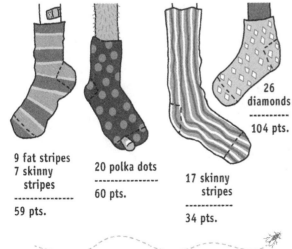

9 fat stripes
7 skinny
   stripes
----
59 pts.

20 polka dots
----
60 pts.

17 skinny
   stripes
----
34 pts.

26
diamonds
----
104 pts.

page 17 • Dust and Decay

page 18 • Vomit Vocab

THROW UP

TOSS COOKIES

BARF -K+F

H+ ...-C HURL

CHUCK

#1+ OPPOSITE OF ME + -Y PUKE

UPCHUCK

SNAKE NOISE + #1 + FEMALE SHEEP SPEW

BLOW CHUNKS

O	S	T	O	B	S	S	R	F	A	B	T	R
S	P	H	B	L	O	C	H	U	N	K	O	I
M	W	R	O	O	H	F	R	U	H	C	P	D
I	E	P	U	W	O	R	H	T	L	U	S	E
S	P	O	C	C	U	A	B	P	K	H	S	T
S	U	W	H	H	R	B	L	E	U	C	C	H
O	E	L	R	U	H	A	O	W	K	P	O	E
R	K	U	U	N	L	R	W	B	F	U	O	P
G	S	P	Y	K	O	O	C	L	B	P	K	O
B	T	O	S	S	C	O	O	K	I	E	S	R

page 19 • True or False

1. You have as many hairs on your body as a gorilla.
   TRUE or FALSE
2. Your skull protects your brain so it can't be bruised.
   TRUE or **FALSE**
3. Cracking your knuckles can lead to arthritis.
   TRUE or FALSE
4. If you hold in a burp, it will become a fart.
   TRUE or **FALSE**
5. Boogers are very clean.
   TRUE or **FALSE**
6. Fresh spit is cleaner than fresh pee.
   TRUE or **FALSE**
7. The scientific name for snot is mucus.
   TRUE or FALSE
8. You will shed 40 pounds of skin in your lifetime.
   TRUE or FALSE

page 19 • Grossly Gifted

$$4 + 6 - 5\frac{1}{2} = \underline{4\frac{1}{2}}$$

$$7 - 6 + \frac{1}{2} - 2 = \underline{-\frac{1}{2}}$$

$$3 + 1\frac{1}{2} - 4\frac{1}{2} = \underline{0}$$

$$6 - 4\frac{1}{2} + 1 = \underline{2\frac{1}{2}}$$

$$9\frac{1}{2} - 8 - \frac{1}{2} = \underline{1}$$

Total inches = $\underline{7\frac{1}{2}}$

page 21 • What Smells?

Stinky: These pills I got to get rid of B.O. don't work.

Pinky: Why not?

Stinky: They keep falling out from under my arms!

page 22 • Acne Art

PUZZLE ANSWERS

page 23 • Pus-itively Putrid

WVZW	YZXGVIRZ,	WVZW	DSRGV
DEAD	**BACTERIA,**	**DEAD**	**WHITE**

YOLLW	XVOOH,	ZMW	WVZW	YLWB
BLOOD	**CELLS,**	**AND**	**DEAD**	**BODY**

XVOOH	UOLZGRMT	RM	YLWB	UOFRW
CELLS	**FLOATING**	**IN**	**BODY**	**FLUID**

page 23 • How did the teen with acne . . .

HE BROKE OUT!

page 24 • Nasty Rashes

1. Places where bees live

   HIVES

2. Popular poultry + saucepan
   - 20th letter + letter 3rd from end

   CHICKEN POX

3. Killer chemical + 9th letter
   + letter 5th from end

   POISON I V (ivy)

4. Finger jewelry + wiggly bait

   RING WORM

5. A little stick from a needle + LY
   + 8th letter + consume food

   PRICKLY HEAT

page 26 • Hurry Up!

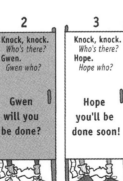

1	2	3	4	5
Knock, knock. *Who's there?* Ben. *Ben who?*	Knock, knock. *Who's there?* Gwen. *Gwen who?*	Knock, knock. *Who's there?* Hope. *Hope who?*	Knock, knock. *Who's there?* Anita. *Anita who?*	Knock, knock. *Who's there?* Harriet. *Harriet who?*
Ben waiting a really long time!	**Gwen will you be done?**	**Hope you'll be done soon!**	**Anita the toilet RIGHT NOW!**	**Harriet up in there!**

page 27 • More Stink Pinks

A bunch of boy scouts all going #2 at the same time

TROOP POOP

Tiny tinkle

WEE PEE

Long time you sat when constipated

GREAT WAIT

Fast press of the toilet handle

RUSH FLUSH

Line of poop on the toilet paper

WIPE STRIPE

When you accidentally throw up on your mom's fancy clothes

DRESS MESS

page 27 • What kind of Nasty Nuts . . .

B P F E H J E H
N H U F B O T
M B H F M R S
G V A M R J G
O V M C J V N
F H D M J R R
G F C O R V L F
M E C V O G J
A G B C F H K
G C H S B V O

PEENUTS AND LEAKS!
(PEANUTS AND LEEKS)

PUZZLE ANSWERS

page 28 • Constipation

3 LETTERS: can, tan, pan, pat, tap, nap, cap, cat, pin, nip, pit, tip, tin, sin, ton, son, top, pot, cot, cop

4 LETTERS: coat, coin, stop, pant, cost, post, past, cast, snip, spin, snap, span, pain

5 LETTERS: paint, stain, patio, point, onion, stoop

6 LETTERS: notion, potion, nation, station

page 29 • Why did the toilet paper...

You start with the second letter "T" from the end of the roll.

page 30 • Silly Sentences

<u>F</u>reddy <u>f</u>arted <u>f</u>ifty <u>f</u>ast <u>f</u>umes.

<u>P</u>eter <u>p</u>ooped <u>p</u>artly <u>p</u>ointy <u>p</u>ieces.

<u>V</u>ictor <u>v</u>omited <u>v</u>ery <u>v</u>iolet <u>v</u>itamins.

<u>T</u>herese <u>t</u>inkled <u>t</u>welve <u>t</u>iny <u>t</u>imes.

<u>B</u>illy <u>b</u>lew <u>b</u>lue <u>b</u>oogers <u>b</u>ackwards.

<u>S</u>teven <u>s</u>pit <u>s</u>oggy <u>s</u>unflower <u>s</u>eeds.

page 30 • How do two pieces of "number 2"...

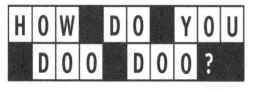

HOW DO YOU DOO DOO?

page 32 • Run! Run! Run!

A step on a ladder	R U N <u>G</u>
Smallest one in a litter	R U N <u>T</u>
What a model walks down	R U N <u>W</u> <u>A</u> Y
Someone who likes to run	R U N N <u>E</u> R
Breakfast and lunch combo	B R U N C <u>H</u>
Past tense of drink	D R U N <u>K</u>
Dirty and messy	G R U N G <u>Y</u>
A noisy, crackling chew	C R U N <u>C</u> H
A fruit that helps you poop	P R U N <u>E</u>
Main stem of a tree	T R U N <u>K</u>
Short, deep sound	G R U N <u>T</u>
To play again	R <u>E</u> R U N

page 32 • What is white, full of poop,...

Turn the book on its side when you hold it up to the mirror, and tip the top edge slight back toward you. Then you should be clearly able to read the answer "A TOY-LET"!

page 33 • Target Practice

The puddle each guy makes matches the shape on his head. So each of Pete's puddles has four blobby "arms," Pablo's puddles have five, and Perry's puddles have three.

Pete
$$70 - 10 = 60$$
1 puddle on floor

Pablo
$$80 + 15 - 20 = 75$$
direct hit — 2 puddles on floor

Perry
$$60 + 20 = 80$$
bonus for no puddles on floor

PUZZLE ANSWERS

page 34 • Why did that guy . . .

Why did that guy bring toilet paper to a birthday party?

B E C A U S E
H E S A
P A R T Y
P O O P E R !

A. Robe worn by superheroes
C A P E
3 4 20 21

B. Autumn fruit
P E A R
12 7 11 14

C. Meat or veggies cooked in broth
S O U P
6 18 5 17

D. To annoy
B O T H E R
1 19 15 8 2 22

E. Not hard
E A S Y
9 13 10 16

page 35 • Gotta Go

1. <u>NATURE</u> <u>CALLS</u>
2. <u>TAKE</u> <u>A</u> <u>LEAK</u>
3. <u>GOT</u> <u>TO</u> <u>PEE</u>
4. <u>TAKE</u> <u>A</u> <u>WHIZ</u>
5. <u>FILL</u> <u>THE</u> <u>CAN</u>
6. <u>GO</u> <u>TO</u> <u>THE</u> <u>JOHN</u>
7. <u>HIT</u> <u>THE</u> <u>HEAD</u>

page 35 • It's the Rule!

I DON'T SWIM IN YOUR TOILET, SO DON'T PEE IN MY POOL!

page 36 • Bathroom Pass

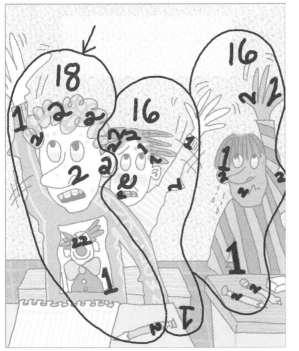

page 38 • The Putrid Painter

page 39 • **What is long and pointy . . .**

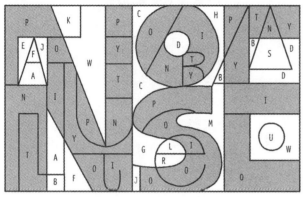

page 39 • **Baby Brother B.O.**

Lance   Luke   Leo   Larry   Lenny

page 40 • **How can you tell if . . .**

A. A good time
F U N
18 9 4

D. Number after eight
N I N E
10 2 13 20

B. Happy faces have these
S M I L E S
6 23 16 25 7 11

E. Decays
R O T S
8 5 21 22

C. To make better
H E A L S
1 19 12 26 17

F. Small storage building
S H E D
3 15 24 14

1C	2D	3F		4A	5E	6B	7B
H	I	S		N	O	S	E
8E	**9A**	**10D**	**11B**		**12C**	**13D**	**14F**
R	U	N	S		A	N	D
15F	**16B**	**17C**		**18A**	**19C**	**20D**	**21E**
H	I	S		F	E	E	T
22E	**23B**	**24F**	**25B**	**26C**			
S	M	E	L	L	!		

page 41 • **Juicy Jobs?**

TROPA-TOPTY NEALCER	PORTA-POTTY CLEANER
EPT DOOF STERAT	PET FOOD TASTER
OPOP YALSTAN	POOP ANALYST
REWES VIRED	SEWER DIVER
IRAMPT RFISNFE	ARMPIT SNIFFER

page 42 •
Uncle Leon's Lovely Leg

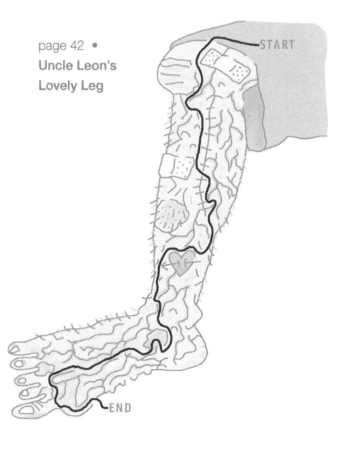

START

END

PUZZLE ANSWERS

page 42 •
Just Joking!

1. PAT
2. BILL
3. ART
4. JACK
5. RUSSELL
6. MATT

page 43 •
Scritch Scratch

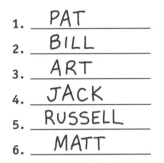

1. F **A R M P I T** I
2. **S C A L P** O P
3. E **N O S E** A T
4. B E L **C H I N** N
5. L U O **N E C K** K
6. **B A C K** S I D
7. E R **C H E S T** T
8. O **B U T T** E N
9. T H **A R M** E T
10. S L E **L E G** I G E
11. E S **T O E** N O
12. R U **B E L L Y** L Y

page 44 • Bob's Bad Body Noises

BELCH	3
FART	8
GAG	16
GRUNT	3
GULP	4
RETCH	2
SNIFF	4
SNORT	4

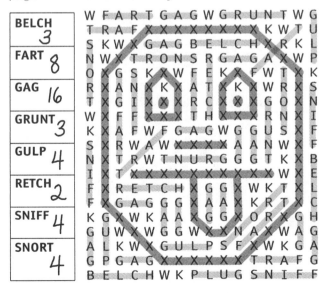

page 45 • Very Funny, Grandpa!

START GRAND	CHILD	LIKE	WISE	MEN
MOTHER	BIRTH	DOWN	RIGHT	HORSE
HOOD	DAY	BREAK	HAND	CLOTH
ON	TIME	TABLE	OUT	HOUSE END

Answer to "Grandpa's Cooking": The joke reads normally from left to right "What's the difference between Grandpa's cooking and a pile of slugs?" The answer to the joke is written between the lines. It is backwards and can be read if you hold the book up to a mirror. "Grandpa's cooking usually comes with a knife and a fork!"

page 46 • Family Photos

page 46 • What do you call your cousin . . .

G	R	E	E	N	S	L	E	E	V	E	S

page 48 • **What did the monster mama say . . .**

STOP PICKING YOUR NOSES!

page 50 • **Losing Lunch**

Everyone's story will be different. Here's a sample:

(_MONDAY_) I had a (_GOOEY_) stomach
_{day of the week} _{awful adjective}
ache. I don't know why! At lunch I only ate (_47_)
_{big number}
(_PIZZAS_) and (_312_)(_TWINKIES_).
_{food item, plural} _{big number} _{different food item, plural}
For dessert I had (_1,201_) (_RAISINS_). By the time I
_{number} _{food item, plural}
got home, I felt (_MOLDY_). My stomach started
_{awful adjective}
(_JUMPING_) and my face turned (_AQUA_). I ran for the
_{action word} _{color}
bathroom, but my (_STICKY_) brother, (_ALFRED_),
_{awful adjective} _{boy's name}
was in there. Sometimes he stays

in there for (_32_) hours.
_{big number}
Oh no! So I ran into the

(_LAUNDRY ROOM_), instead,
_{room in your house, not the bathroom}
and threw up in a (_PENCIL HOLDER_).
_{container}
I felt much better after that!

page 51 • **Yum! Bugs!**

```
W E Y L F N O G A R D H G
A T E K C I R C T D O Y U
O I U C I C A D A G E T B
I M F A N T B Y O U N C K
G R R T O S E S M R O W N
U E A E T E E R M I I T I
B T A R A N T U L A P G T
R E W P I T L H A B R O S
E O K I A N E I N U O S P
T E C L T T H A B T C E I
A S I L K W O R M A S T D
W S I A T S O W N W O R E
D S G R A S S H O P P E R
```

WHAT DO YOU GET IF YOU CROSS A
TERMITE WITH A BOOK? AN INSECT
THAT EATS ITS OWN WORDS!

page 52 • **Waiter! There's a fly in my soup!**

1.	2.	3.	4.
Be quiet, or everyone will want one!	That's OK! There's enough for both of you!	Yes, they really like rotten food!	Oops! That's yesterday's soup. Today's soup has a beetle!

PUZZLE ANSWERS

page 53 • Clean the Fridge!

C	R	U	S	T	Y
Y	U	C	K	Y	
	F	I	Z	Z	Y
S	M	E	L	L	Y
	N	A	S	T	Y
R	A	N	C	I	D
	F	E	T	I	D

G	R	E	E	N	
T	O	X	I	C	
	P	U	T	R	I	D
R	O	T	T	E	N
S	C	A	R	Y	
O	O	Z	I	N	G
	M	O	L	D	Y
W	E	I	R	D	
S	T	I	N	K	Y
V	O	M	I	T	O	U	S
S	L	I	M	Y	

page 54 • Peanut Butter and . . .?

<u>**B**O**LOG**N</u>A
<u>**P**OTA**T**O **C**HIP**S**</u>
<u>**C**HO**C**O**L**</u>ATE
<u>**B**A**C**O**N**</u>
<u>**C**HEE**S**E</u>
<u>**P**I**C**K**L**E**S**</u>
<u>**M**U**S**TA**R**D</u>
<u>**P**AR**SL**E**Y**</u>
<u>**M**A**Y**O**NN**A</u>ISE
<u>**O**NI**O**N</u>
<u>B.**B**.Q. **S**A**U**C**E**</u>

page 55 • Gag Man, Glad Man

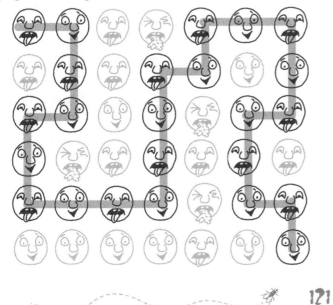

121

page 56 • Lose Your Appetite

page 59 • To Market

1 P.H. (with big ears)
PIG HEAD
4 D.F. (clean webbing)
DUCK FEET
3 F. (good jumpers)
FROGS
4 T. (with all 8 legs)
TARANTULAS
1 S. (watch stinger)
SCORPION
15 W. (wiggly)
WORMS
2 G. (necks 9 inches)
GEESE

page 57 • Bug Eater

B	E	D
O	N	E
A	T	E
H	O	T
U	M	P
D	O	G
A	P	E
S	H	E
M	A	D
A	G	E
E	Y	E

page 57 • Delicious Delicacies

Milk-giver's smart parts
COW BRAINS

Cud chewer's mouth muscle
COW TONGUE

Hopper's essential parts
FROG LEGS

Baa baa's tum tum
SHEEP STOMACH

Ape's kissing equipment
MONKEY LIPS

Porker's walkers
PIG FEET

page 60 • The Barf Buffet

XLFTS-VV
COUGH-EE

STENCH FRIES

EBOESVGG
DANDRUFF
GMZLFT
FLAKES

AKEC FO
CAKE OF
OAPS
SOAP

page 62 • White stuff from the sky?

1Q N	2M E	3H V	4P E	5N R		6C C	7P A	8N T	9F C	10D H
11H S	12D N	13G O	14A W	15L F		16K L	17Q A	18F K	19A E	20J S
21D W	22A I	23A T	24A H			25Q Y	26H O	27N U	28P R	
29P T	30M O	31Q N	32G G	33C U	34D E		35I U	36Q N	37R T	38D I	39C L
	40E A	41L L	42M L		43B T	44B H	45J E				
46F B	47I I	48C R	49B D	50I S		51K H	52F A	53M V	54J E	
55M G	56L O	57E N	58K E		59P S	60L O	61B U	62I T	63O H	
64G F	65R O	66E R		67O T	68N H	69K E				
70R W	71O I	72O N	73H T	74H E	75G R	!				

NEVER CATCH SNOWFLAKES WITH YOUR TONGUE UNTIL ALL THE BIRDS HAVE GONE SOUTH FOR THE WINTER!

A. Opposite of black
W H I T E
14 24 22 23 19

B. A heavy, dropping sound
T H U D
43 44 61 49

C. To wind around
C U R L
6 33 48 39

D. High, complaining voice
W H I N E
21 10 38 12 34

E. Past tense of run
R A N
66 40 57

F. Opposite of front
B A C K
46 52 9 18

G. Toad's relative
F R O G
64 75 13 32

H. Casts a ballot
V O T E S
3 26 73 74 11

I. Pants and jacket combo
S U I T
50 35 47 62

J. Take in with the eyes
S E E
20 45 54

K. Rear part of a foot
H E E L
51 58 69 16

L. To trick
F O O L
15 56 60 41

M. Winter hand covering
G L O V E
55 42 30 53 2

N. To injure
H U R T
68 27 5 8

O. Not fat
T H I N
67 63 71 72

P. Look at for a long time
S T A R E
59 29 7 28 4

Q. Live-in babysitter
N A N N Y
36 17 1 31 25

R. Number before three
T W O
37 70 65

page 64 • A Creature's Gotta Eat

i Shove my StomAcH out thRough my mouth and surround what i'm eaTing. i pull It back in when i'm Full.

STARFISH

i tHrow up On Food, and thE acid turns mY meaL to soUp. then i Slurp it up!

HOUSEFLY

i liVe by eating animals thaT are alReady dead. the eye-balLs are easy to get to, so it is not UnusUal that i Eat them first.

VULTURE

i attaCh to my dinnEr's skin and suck bLood up to ninE times my weigHt.

LEECH

i crush an animal uNtil it stoPs breathing. then i unHook my jaws and stretch mY mouth exTra wide. this lets me swallow my dinner whOle!

PYTHON

page 65 • Doo They, or Don't They?

Rabbits	(YES)	NO
Cats	YES	(NO)
Dogs	(YES)	NO
Koalas	(YES)	NO

page 65 • Those Dang Beetles

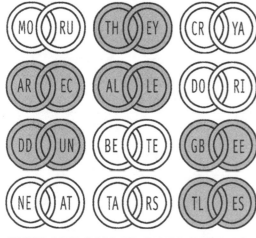

MO RU | TH EY | CR YA
AR EC | AL LE | DO RI
DD UN | BE TE | GB EE
NE AT | TA RS | TL ES

These beetles collect and roll balls of dung, or poop, in which to lay their eggs. They also eat dung for dinner!

THEY ARE CALLED DUNG BEETLES

page 66 • ICK! That's what makes me sneeze?!?

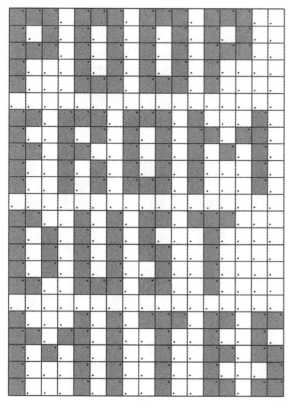

A DUST MITE IS A DISTANT RELATIVE OF THE SPIDER. IT IS A TINY CRITTER TOO SMALL TO SEE WITHOUT A POWERFUL MICROSCOPE. DUST MITES LIVE BY EATING THE MILLIONS OF DEAD SKIN CELLS YOU SHED ALL OVER THE HOUSE EACH DAY.

page 67 • Open Wide

TURTLE

DEER

TOAD

OWL

FISH

MOUSE

page 67 • Nice Cow?

Cows ~~chew~~ have ~~chew~~ trouble ~~chew~~ digesting ~~chew~~ the ~~chew~~ grass ~~chew~~ they ~~chew~~ eat ~~chew~~. They ~~chew~~ chew ~~chew~~ and ~~chew~~ swallow ~~chew~~ grass ~~chew~~ in ~~chew~~ the ~~chew~~ field ~~chew~~. Later ~~chew~~, they ~~chew~~ upchuck ~~chew~~ the ~~chew~~ partially ~~chew~~ digested ~~chew~~ grass ~~chew~~ and ~~chew~~ rechew ~~chew~~ it ~~chew~~ — for ~~chew~~ up ~~chew~~ to ~~chew~~ 9 ~~chew~~ hours ~~chew~~ a ~~chew~~ day ~~chew~~!

page 68 • **Shark Bite**

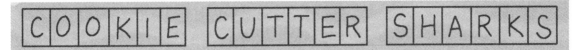

COOKIE CUTTER SHARKS

page 69 • **Big Monkeys**

B A - B O O M S !

page 69 • **Elephant Nose Pick**

T	H	E	Y		D	O	N	'	T		K	N	O	W
	W	H	E	R	E		T	O		H	I	D	E	
A		T	W	O		F	O	O	T		L	O	N	G
	B	O	O	G	E	R	!							

page 70 • **It's Not Snot**

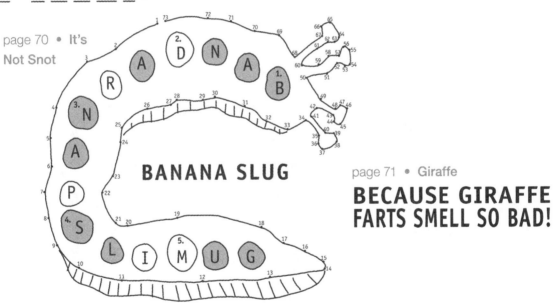

BANANA SLUG

page 71 • **Giraffe**

BECAUSE GIRAFFE FARTS SMELL SO BAD!

page 72 • **Slobber = ?**

On a hot day, a dog uses its tongue to...

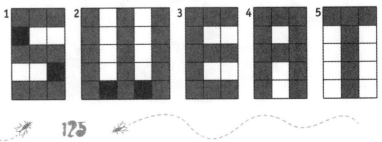

PUZZLE ANSWERS

page 74 • Watch Your Step

A. Not a special one
$\underline{A}_{10}$ $\underline{N}_{11}$ $\underline{Y}_{9}$

B. Cow noise
$\underline{M}_{13}$ $\underline{O}_{17}$ $\underline{O}_{18}$

C. Opposite of work
$\underline{P}_{19}$ $\underline{L}_{15}$ $\underline{A}_{14}$ $\underline{Y}_{4}$

D. Center of a peach
$\underline{P}_{16}$ $\underline{I}_{12}$ $\underline{T}_{6}$

E. Opposite of she
$\underline{H}_{2}$ $\underline{E}_{3}$

F. Tiny bits of dirt
$\underline{D}_{8}$ $\underline{U}_{7}$ $\underline{S}_{5}$ $\underline{T}_{1}$

page 74 • Hey, Hippo!

MALE HIPPOS WILL TURN BUTT TO BUTT AND SPRAY EACH OTHER WITH A GLOPPY MIXTURE OF POOP AND URINE!

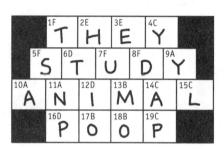

THEY STUDY ANIMAL POOP

page 75 • Feed Me

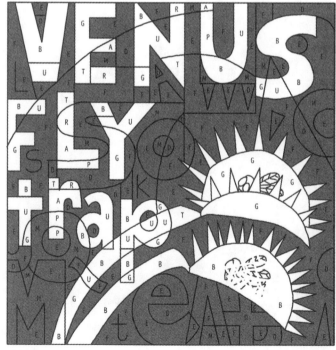

VENUS FLY Trap

page 76 • Yucky Yucky

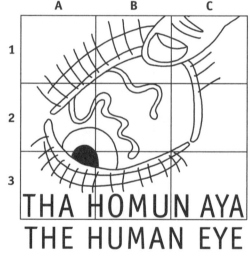

THA HOMUN AYA
THE HUMAN EYE

page 77 • Monster Eyes

PARIS, BECAUSE THE EYE-FULL TOWER IS THERE!

page 78 • Attack Plant

1. Opposite of "Hi!"
B Y E

2. Night before
E V E

3. Fake hair
W I G

4. Number before two
O N E

5. What a ghost says
B O O

6. To request
A S K

7. Opposite of lose
W I N

8. Mama pig
S O W

9. Monkey relative
A P E

1.	2.	3.		4.	5.	6.	7.	8.	9.
Y	V	I		N	O	S	I	O	P

If you read the answer the correct way, it's POISON IVY.

page 79 • Smelly Letters

Q **B** I S X C S **O** J
L T C **A** M T C X Y
R W E I R Y **N** Z J
Z T J **D** Q T E I M
S **P** I E X **U** L W C I

B.O. AND P.U.

page 80 • Where's the Gross?

1. The kid(s lug)ged four cans of garbage.
2. The (slim e)arthworm poops in the dirt.
3. While belchin(g, Ross) can also chant.
4. Joe(s pit) bull was chewin(g a g)reasy bone.
5. The secon(ret ch)ain opens the dirty drain.
6. Does anyone eat warthog(g or e)lectric eel?
7. Bob(s not)e was dumb and disgusting.

page 80 • Why was the pig farmer . . .

HE	~~FOE~~	WAS	~~THINK~~
~~TANK~~	THANKFUL	~~SEA~~	~~FOG~~
THAT	~~FORGETFUL~~	PIGS	~~RANK~~
~~TEA~~	CAN'T	~~FEE~~	FLY

He was thankful that pigs can't fly!

page 79 • How Many Farts

J U S T   A   P H E W!

PUZZLE ANSWERS

page 81 • Sloppy Sentences

Seven slimy slugs slid softly sideways.

Gary's greasy guts grew green garbage.

Big black bugs bleed black blood.

Foul feces flopped from five flatworms.

Many maggots make moist meals messy.

page 82 • Gross Gulps

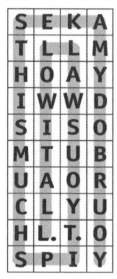

Your body makes this much spit. You swallow it all.

page 83 • Got Maggots?

JUGGLER
FOGGY
DRAGGED
EGGROLL
HUGGED
BIGGER
GIGGLE
BAGGAGE
WIGGLE
SUGGEST
NUGGET

page 84 • Terribly Tiny

AROUND THE

ROOTS OF YOUR

EYELASHES.

YES, YOURS!

page 86 • Ouch!

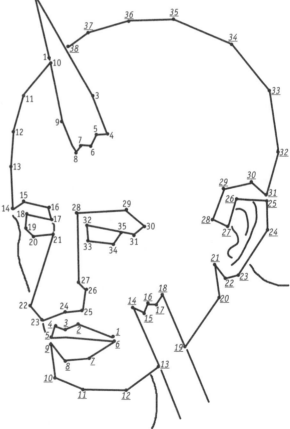

page 87 • Awfully Ancient

R	N	X	U	X	M	X	X	B	N	X	E	X	X	S	S	X
X	R	B	O	X	T	X	T	E	X	N	X	N	X	O	S	E
Y	E	X	L	X	L	O	X	W	X	B	X	U	X	M	P	X	S
X	T	X	H	I	X	C	M	K	X	E	M	A	R	M	S	X	M
S	X	T	I	X	F	F	X	E	X	Y	E	X	L	I	X	D	S
N	X	O	M	F	X	R	O	X	N	T	M	T	E	X	E	T	H
X	D	E	X	F	O	R	X	M	E	X	D	T	O	X	E	S	X
L	O	X	S	X	S	O	X	F	F	X	I	N	G	X	X	R	S

page 87 • Nail Biter

WEAR YOUR SHOES!

page 88 •
Seriously
Surgical

A decade is ? years	10
Cards in a deck	52
A score is ? years	20
Twelve pairs of shoes	24
Fingers on two hands	10
A gross equals ? items	144
Eighty quarters is ? dollars	20
An egg carton holds ? eggs	12
Two cups of butter is ? sticks	4
There are ? days in a year	365
There are ? keys on the piano	88
Number of pennies in a dollar	100
Ten gallons of milk is ? quarts	40
An octogenarian is ? years old	80
Number of pits in an avocado	1

TOTAL 970

page 88 • Awful Smell

So would I!
(Sew wood eye!)

page 89 • Almost Everybody Gets It

A little hot = W A R M
Foot digit = T O E
Stand-up bath = S H O W E R
Body dryer = T O W E L
Opposite of dry = W E T
Scratch this = I T C H
To perspire = S W E A T
Foot bottom = S O L E
No foot cover = B A R E F O O T
Soft foot cover = S O C K
Hard foot cover = S H O E
Barely wet = M O I S T

page 89 • Swallowed Pen

USE A PENCIL TIL I GET THERE!

page 90 •
Sticky Solution

page 90 • **Run Down**

The license plate number of the car that hit you!

page 91 • **Rhinowhat?**

A CLOSE LOOK
DEEP INSIDE
THE NOSE

look deep
the a inside nose
close

and yellow
the nose
of
from flow liquid
green

picking

nose constant

You must stop that
RHINOTILLEXOMANIA
while I do a
RHINOSCOPY
to look more
closely at your
RHINORRHEA!

FLOW OF YELLOW
AND GREEN LIQUID
FROM THE NOSE

CONSTANT
NOSE
PICKING

page 91 • **Nose Apart**

I WANTED TO SEE WHAT MADE IT RUN!

PUZZLE ANSWERS

page 92 • Body Sculpting

A LONG METAL
TUBE IS STUCK
UNDER THE
SKIN AND FAT
IS SUCKED OUT

page 92 • Brain Surgeon

I was a dentist until my drill slipped!

page 93 • Slimy Helpers

page 93 • Biting Insects

STOP BITING THEM!

page 94 • Where does Mrs. Doctor keep . . .

1F S	2F H	3B E		4A K	5C E	6F E	7A P	8F S
9E T	10B H	11A E	12D M		13E I	14B N		15E H	16A E	17C R
18D H	19C A	20E N	21F D	22C B	23D A	24C G !

A. To continue to have
K E E P
4 11 16 7

B. A female chicken
H E N
10 3 14

C. Boat with a flat bottom
B A R G E
22 19 17 24 5

D. Meat from a pig
H A M
18 23 12

E. Opposite of fat
T H I N
9 15 13 20

F. Small storage buildings
S H E D S
8 2 6 21 1

page 94 • First Surgery

Surgeon: I know just how you feel. This is the first time I've done any!

131

page 95 • "I don't feel very good . . ."

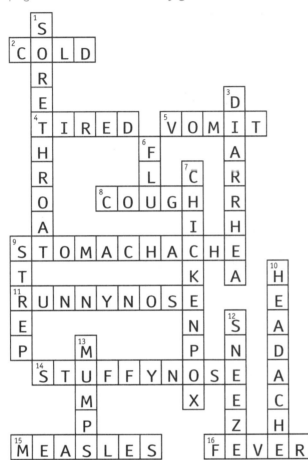

page 96 • Really Rotten

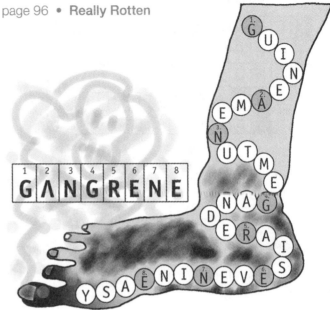

GANGRENE

page 98 • Zombie
Newspaper Article

THE DAILY POOP
TOILET
NEWS
PAPER

ZOMBIE LOSES MARATHON BY WIDE MARGIN

After quite a lively start, zombie athlete, Fester N. Rott, was dismayed to finish the race dead last.

page 95 • Double Vision

Your vision is fine. The problem is you have two heads!

page 96 • Headache

Yes! Crash your head through that window and the pane will be gone!

PUZZLE ANSWERS

page 98 • What's the last thing . . .

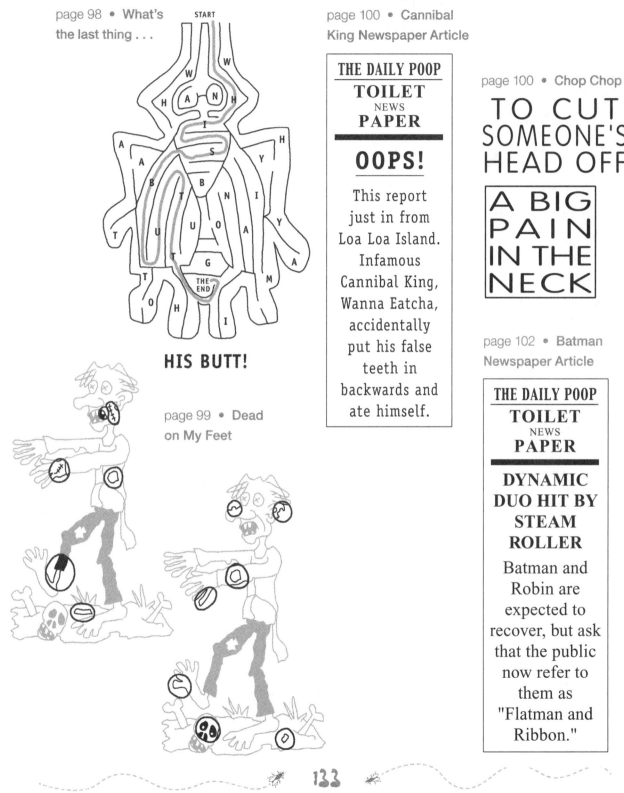

START

HIS BUTT!

page 99 • Dead on My Feet

page 100 • Cannibal King Newspaper Article

> ## THE DAILY POOP
> ### TOILET
> #### NEWS
> ### PAPER
>
> ---
>
> ## OOPS!
>
> This report just in from Loa Loa Island. Infamous Cannibal King, Wanna Eatcha, accidentally put his false teeth in backwards and ate himself.

page 100 • Chop Chop

TO CUT SOMEONE'S HEAD OFF

A BIG PAIN IN THE NECK

page 102 • Batman Newspaper Article

> ## THE DAILY POOP
> ### TOILET
> #### NEWS
> ### PAPER
>
> ---
>
> ### DYNAMIC DUO HIT BY STEAM ROLLER
>
> Batman and Robin are expected to recover, but ask that the public now refer to them as "Flatman and Ribbon."

PUZZLE ANSWERS

page 102 • **Dead Poet's Society**

SEVEN SNEAKER **DEAD** VOMIT **MAN ON THE BRIDGE** ONE **LAST NIGHT,** POOP **HIS** CLOG **BONES WERE** THREE **ALL** EARWAX **AQUIVER.** HE SPIT **GAVE A** FART COUGH, HIS BOOT **LEG** FOOT **FELL** YUCK **OFF,** SANDAL **AND FLOATED** FIVE **DOWN** POOP **THE** BUTT HEAD **RIVER!**

page 103 • **Mummy Mia!**

1. Body is _____D_____ on the left side.

2. Lungs, liver, stomach, and intestine_____G_____.

3. The brain is _____E_____.

4. The heart is the only organ _____C_____.

5. The inside of the body is _____F_____.

6. Body is _____A_____ and left to dry for two months.

7. Body is_____B_____ that comes from trees.

8. _____H_____ sand, sawdust, and cloth.

9. Body is _____I_____ in linen bandages.

page 104 • **Karate Newspaper Article**

THE DAILY POOP
TOILET
NEWS
PAPER

KAR OUCH ATE
EXP OUCH ERT
KNO OUCH CKED
O OUCH UT
FIR OUCH ST
DA OUCH Y
I OUCH N
AR OUCH MY

Pri ouch vate B ouch. Be ouch lt w ouch as pract ouch icing ho ouch w t ouch o sal ouch ute.

page 104 • **Hangman's Holiday**

2. THE [image: fish] C

The Dead Sea

1. THE [image: noose] +PAPER

The noose-paper (newspaper)

3. [image: face] +TARINES

Neck-tarines (Nectarines)

page 106 • **Indian Chief Newspaper Article**

THE DAILY POOP
TOILET
NEWS
PAPER

INDIAN CHIEF DIES IN STRANGE ACCIDENT

Chief Hot Mug reportedly drank fifteen cups of tea before going to bed last night. He was found this morning, drowned in his own tea-pee.

PUZZLE ANSWERS

page 106 • **What does the headstone say . . .**

HE RESTS
IN PIECES

page 108 • **Dead End**

Rotten bananas are very B E N D A B L E.

Would you really eat a bug, or just P R E T E N D to?

A true F R I E N D will L E N D you his whoopie cushion.

Would you S P E N D your money on garlic gum or earwax candy?

A boring monster movie seems E N D L E S S.

A really gross joke might O F F E N D your grandma.

Some things should <u>not</u> go in a B L E N D E R.

The gross cook R E C O M M E N D S the scorpion soup.

page 107 • Mad Scientist Newspaper Article

THE DAILY POOP
TOILET
NEWS
PAPER

MAD SCIENTIST TURNS INTO FROG

Doctor Greenblood's mother was quoted as saying "I told him never to lick the spoon after mixing a new potion!"

page 109 • Look Again!

1. It Was The Dog!

2. How did the teen...

3. Why did the t.p. ...

4. Juicy Jobs?

5. Clean the Fridge!

6. Giraffe

7. Why was the pig farmer...

8. Rhinowhat?

9. Chop Chop

The Everything® KIDS' Series!

Packed with tons of information, activities, and puzzles, the Everything® Kids' books are perennial bestsellers that keep kids active and engaged.

Each book is two-color, 8" x 9¼", and 144 pages.

All this at the incredible price of $6.95!

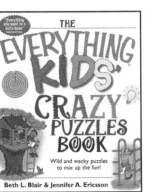

The Everything® Kids' Crazy
Puzzles Book
1-59337-361-9

The Everything® Kids'
Dinosaurs Book
1-59337-360-0

A silly, goofy, and undeniably icky addition to
the Everything® Kids' series . . .

The Everything® Kids'

GROSS
Series

Chock-full of sickening entertainment for hours of disgusting fun.

The Everything® Kids' Gross
Jokes Book
1-59337-448-8

The Everything® Kids' Gross
Puzzle & Activity Book
1-59337-447-X

Other Everything® Kids' Titles Available

The Everything® Kids' Animal Puzzle & Activity Book
1-59337-305-8

The Everything® Kids' Baseball Book, 3rd Ed.
1-59337-070-9

The Everything® Kids' Bible Trivia Book
1-59337-031-8

The Everything® Kids' Bugs Book
1-58062-892-3

The Everything® Kids' Christmas Puzzle &
Activity Book
1-58062-965-2

The Everything® Kids' Cookbook
1-58062-658-0

The Everything® Kids' Halloween Puzzle &
Activity Book
1-58062-959-8

The Everything® Kids' Hidden Pictures Book
1-59337-128-4

The Everything® Kids' Joke Book
1-58062-686-6

The Everything® Kids' Knock Knock Book
1-59337-127-6

The Everything® Kids' Math Puzzles Book
1-58062-773-0

The Everything® Kids' Mazes Book
1-58062-558-4

The Everything® Kids' Money Book
1-58062-685-8

The Everything® Kids' Nature Book
1-58062-684-X

The Everything® Kids' Puzzle Book
1-58062-687-4

The Everything® Kids' Riddles
& Brain Teasers Book
1-59337-036-9

The Everything® Kids' Science Experiments Book
1-58062-557-6

The Everything® Kids' Sharks Book
1-59337-304-X

The Everything® Kids' Soccer Book
1-58062-642-4

The Everything® Kids' Travel Activity Book
1-58062-641-6